UB Law and Political Science Quarterly

University of Buea

UB Law and Political Science Quarterly

A publication of the Faculty of Laws and Political Science

Vol. 3, N° 1, July 2023

L'Harmattan
Cameroun

5-7, rue de l'Ecole-Polytechnique, 75005 Paris

http://www.editions-harmattan.fr

ISBN : 978-2-336-43694-4
EAN : 9782336436944

Prof Monkam Cyrille
Prof Jean-Didier Boukongou, Catholic University of Central Africa
Prof Tabe Simon, University of Dschang
Prof Hansungule, Centre for Human Rights, University of Pretoria
Prof Pierre-Etienne Kenfack, University of Yaoundé II
Prof Gabsa Wilfred, University of Yaoundé II
Prof Cosmas Cheka, University of Yaoundé II
Prof Enyinna Nwauche, Nelson Mandela school of Law, University of Fort Hare
Prof Frans Viljoen, Centre for Human Rights, University of Pretoria
Prof Amadou Monkare, University of Dschang
Justice Alexis Ndzuenkeu, Chief of Service in Charge of Legal Affairs and Communication, OHADA

CONTENTS

Public Policies, Labour and Industrial Relations' Practices and Development or Underdevelopment in Africa's Postcolonial States - A Marxist Analysis

By

Peter Sakwe Masumbe

Associate Professor of Public Administration,
Department of Public Law and Public Administration; University of Buea.
Email: masumbep@yahoo.com

Abstract

This paper examines how elitist public policies on labour and industrial relations in postcolonial Africa's states attenuate development to stimulate underdevelopment therein. It argues that, once labour is attenuated the worker becomes estranged from the production process especially goods/services. It asserts that, labour and industrial relations (L&IR) being the substratum for man's existence, labour starts with policymaking to fashion labour itself and ends in goods, services and consumption. Using Marxist analysis and the elite theory in policymaking, this paper debunks elites' claims to superior knowledge, power and wealth including their imposed preferences upon the masses, politics and economy as imperialism against labour and industrial relations. Herein, L&IR becomes the gratuitous beneficiary of underdevelopment which secure decisive positions for elites for perpetuating social strata that endanger the production process. It chastises the weaknesses of labour economics and human resource management theories inherent in capitalism; and concludes by revealing the inseparability of policies, labour/worker from goods and services; while advocating for masses oriented policies on L&IR.

Key words: Policy, labour, industrial, development, underdevelopment, economy, Marxist, Africa.

Introduction

As most writers note, "...postcolonial African states asphyxiate in vast underdevelopment narratives"1 But such is neither any longer news; nor is it a striking research problem. An attention-grabbing news or research problem could be for instance, to examine the causes and effects of the endemic underdevelopment saga in postcolonial Africa's states; away from the over-flogged culprits – European orchestrated slavery and colonialism.[2] Several decades since self-rules, even these culprits could be exculpated. So, to understand the causes of Africa's underdevelopment, one must understand the characters of public policies churned by nascent Africa's political leaders. Irrefutably, policies are *par excellence*, the most single vital agents of growth or undergrowth, next in eminence only to God. For instance, to understand the character of labour and industrial relations' practices in postcolonial Africa's states, one's best path is through the public policies rolled out in this field by Africa's ruling cliques, using the elite theory.[33]

Arguably, as these policies, which are labour in action, obviously shape labour and industrial relation (L&IR) practices, as L&IR practices shape the level of human cognitive capabilities and the ensuing material conditions and economic factors, hence development or underdevelopment results in societies. As Adebayo,[4] asserts, "given Africa's current underdevelopment, arguably prodded by the West and perpetuated by Africa's nascent punchline political

---

[1] Dumont, R., False Start in Africa, London: Earthscan, 1988

[2] Ake, C., A Political Economy of Africa, London: Longman, 1981

[3] Onimode, B., Imperialism and Underdevelopment in Nigeria, London: Macmillan Press Ltd, 1983

[4] Adebayo, B. D., Development Perspective on Employment Relationship in Africa, Lagos: MECK Books, 2019

leaderships, issues related to articulating development-oriented public policies towards L&IR practices to synchronise increased wealth creation, reduce poverty and accelerate human and material growth in Africa, resonate with trepidations in worrying dimensions; not only to wage-earners but also to the continent's vigilant employers of labour." Chiefly, the wage-earner, referred to by Karl Marx (1818 – 1883)[5] as "the proletariat" has inexplicably undergone untold distortions, from a full-fledged workaholic, to a lethargic non-achiever, who although created into a socio-economic milieu endowed with abundant natural resources lives in abject poverty, with calamitous socio-economic and political alienation.

Thus, the policies outcomes on labour and industrial relations from African leaders continue to thwart and dilute the nobility of human labour power, irrespective of its envious position as the substratum for wealth creation. Obviously, conscientious use of labour mitigates poverty and accelerates development of human and material conditions including economic factors. Consequently, this paper mounts to discern the core beliefs, which characterise the dominant public policy thinking, on labour and industrial relations practices and how this abet Africa's current underdevelopment saga. It argues that, it is sheer mischief for persons in any political, economic or social strata to alienate labour from goods and services, because, cyclically, the whole idea of L&IR starts with policymaking, which creates the character of labour, then ends in goods and services. Undoubtedly, these are inseparable bedfellows with labour being the foremost.

Thus, Marx[6] sharply typifies labour, its utility and preeminence in the production process, including the ignominy associated to the working-class, thus: "[...] those

---

[5] Marx, K., Capital: A Critique of Political Economy Vol.1, Moscow: Progress Publishers, 1986

[6] Max 1886, p.34

individuals in society, who sell or mortgage their labour power for a collateral (usually paltry wages) and who do not own the means of production; and for not owning the means and forces of production, do not receive any enviable share of the product of their labour power: money, goods or services, respect for their labour; and thus become alienated from the products of their atom of energy; are the same people who capitalists either milk to death or banish into poverty." As Marx argues, "[...] although these people are disastrously maltreated by mainstream capitalist societies, they are ultimately the bedrock that propels societies' political, economic and social life, which are eventually the outcomes of policymaking"[7]. Accordingly, this paper proceeds with examining the nexus between the elite theory, labour and industrial relations practices, and the ensuing underdevelopment in postcolonial Africa.

1. Elite theory, L&IR, development and underdevelopment in Africa

As Lenin[8] once said, "...the repulsive character of labour and industrial relations practices in various human societies is lavishly emitted by self-seeking public policies, incarnated by insensitive elites against the masses." Similarly, Damele and Santos[7] note, "...in the last few years, keen attention has been paid to the contrapositions held between the masses and elites, perceived as a fundamental talk of the anti-elitist discourse." Herein, both the masses and the elite supposedly express a conception of a will of homogeneous interest. But criticisms levelled against elitism, typically focus on how their views distort the values and ends of labour democracy,

---

7 Ibid., p.67

8 Lenin, V.I., Imperialism as the Highest Stage of Capitalism, Moscow: Progress Publisher, 1920

especially how it misconstrues the masses through biased policy insinuations.

Certainly, this is not strange, because of the existence of a tradition dating back to the nineteenth century's that sought to identify the internal dynamics of elites against the masses. With changes in societies, which increased franchise in the West, V. Pareto[9], G. Mosca,[10] and R. Michels[11] saw unbridled policy cruelty against the masses.[12]

While insisting that politics is always a game of power struggle in and out of the ruling elite, these authors centred their analysis on the unintended political consequences of rational behaviours, especially by establishing a distinction between the 'rhetoric of legitimation and true motives, which in turn mirrored a more significant and fundamental social distinction between the ruling class and the ruled (per Mosca) or between the elite and the non-elite (per Pareto), all of which arose from policymaking. Definitely, "...democratic elitism played a prominent role in distorting democratisation that took place after the Second World War by providing a conceptual and explanatory framework for the emergence of regimes,"[13] which are exceedingly dependent on well organised, centralised dominant parties, and which primitively appropriated the products of labour, by creating alienated workers' inhuman material conditions and economic factors in societies. Hence, "...this framework and its practical effects has been challenged recently not only by populist political movements but also by theorists of deliberative and

---

9 Vilfredo, P., The Transformation of Democracy, London: Penguin Classics, 1848-1923

10 Gaetano, M., Non Political Classes, New York: Little Brown and Brown, 1858–1941

11 Robert, M., The Iron Law of Oligarchy, London: University of London Press, 1876–1936

12 Yakima, F., Labour Movements, Manpower and Development in Africa, Lagos: JESS Books, 2010

13 Ibid., p. 39

participatory democratic policymaking, who emphasise the direct involvement of citizens in informed processes of collective decision-making, since such movements accuse democratic elitism of being either a perversion of democracy or no democracy at all."[14]

Accordingly, scholars[15] outline, elitism as involving elements, which are anti-labour and growth in Africa, thus:

a) The primary objective of every elites is to preserve power and privilege against any opposing forces.

b) The rule of the elite is based upon force and fraud through policies that reinforce their preferences in societies.

c) The elite social structure is sustained by a political formula that typically must correlate with; and generally be accepted as religion, ideology or myth by the whole society.

d) Every elite has two opposing tendencies: (a) an aristocratic tendency, by which the elitism seeks to preserve the ruling position of its members and to prevent others from entering its ranks; (b) a heretic democratic tendency by which (*i*) new elements force their way into the elite from below or (*ii*) the ruling class self-recycles by absorbing only elements from their ranks.

e) Elites adore undue paradigms shift in their composition and structure in situations of social upheavals.

For Pareto the elite theory is truly premised unto falsehood, and the misuse of labour and industrial relations practices; a view which serves as the primary instrument against the masses. Thus, the choking of labour and industrial

---

14 Ibid., p.40

15 Hirschman, A. O., The Rhetoric of Reaction: Cambridge: The Belknap Press of H. U. Press, 1991

relations practices must never be of concern because of the inner features of elitism. Thus, in most societies power and means of production are held by minority. If labour and industrial relations must survive; even in democratic societies, popular rule must prevail, hence, Marxist resolve on seizing the means of production.[16]

Both Mosca and Pareto tried to translate the simple, but almost obvious, observation that all organised societies consist of a vast majority without any political power, with a small minority of all-power-holders. And as they assert, this represents the object of a true science of undemocratic and misleading politics that is meant to provide profound understanding of how the political class recruits itself, maintains itself in power, recycles and illegitimates power and how this class deprives the masses of their true self-actualisation obtained through their own labour power. Thus, the elite creation and control of labour laws such as Law No 92/0092 of 14th August 1992[17] in Cameroon, like elsewhere in Africa, flourishes theoretically but empirically, such laws demean the character of labour and industrial relations practices between the state, employers and employees, mostly at the detriment of labour – the worker. For example, in Cameroon, despite this law, there is no robust, solid and popularly organised labour/workers' movement, with clear democratic paraphernalia to engage into collective bargaining, enviably progressive social dialogues or any kind of negotiations with the state for the purposes of injecting democracy into labour practices. Said differently, Cameroon, like in most of Africa, except in Nigeria, South Africa, organised and democratic labour movements do not exist as an alternative government, capable of challenging state

---

[16] Lenin, Op. Cit., p.15

[17] Law No 92/0092 of 14th August 1992, Relating to the Labour Code

authorities to address socio-economic and political issues of national interest, especially labour.[18]

2. Marxist Analysis: A Justification

Essentially, this paper seeks to prove that, elitist theory negatively drives labour and industrial relations practices, which in turn shape underdevelopment in Africa. To this end, we adopted the Marxist analysis, because of its capacity to explain phenomena from their causes and consequences. Originating from the annals of the skewed social relations between the state, employers and employees, the analytical philosophical position is that, labour power offers value to industries and the market, which serves as a form of socio-economic outlet of goods and services, but such labour is alienated given the self-seeking public policies foisted unto the workers by elites. Marxism rejects the various political and socio-economic categories and structures that practically appear inequitable but constitute the mainstream trends concerning the forms and modalities of income and expenditure mobilisation, allocation and distribution in societies. It further rejects what it describes as capitalism's policies trends, which have no respect for labour. It suggests that, the management of public affairs, regarding labour and industrial relations practices should be anchored upon soundly articulated democratic policies, epitomising peoples' friendliness and development-oriented. Nonetheless, multiple critiques of the Marxism exist today, which commonly but falsely agree that:[19]

- Labour and capital have historically specific forms of social relations, and that labour is not the source of all wealth;

---

[18] Mosca G, The ruling class New York: McGraw-Hill; 1939, See also Pareto V. The mind and society, New York: Harcourt, Brace & Co; 1935.

[19] Dror, Y., The Capacity to Govern, London: CASS, 1984

- Labour is the other side of the same coin as capital, labour presupposes capital, and capital presupposes labour;
- Labour must be subjected to money, which must be decided by means of production, which goes for the whole economy.
- Labour is a category specific to the mode of production, and gains its composite values only by the caprices of capitalism.
- The individual does not exist in some form of vacuum but is rather enmeshed in social relations of production to diligently serve another person for a wage, as it has been sanctioned by the sovereignty character of the state. But what sovereignty?

Consequently, at the roots of the foregoing, is the revelation that, for Africa to develop, elitism must accept to work with the masses, because try sovereignty belongs to the masses. Africa must possess dedicate individuals with democratic mindsets, grounded in policymaking, attuned to the enviable distinctions of statesmen and women, who preside over what Dror[19] calls, "national and international relations high order tasks," in the management of public affairs, especially in labour and industrial relations, it being the primordial human discipline, through which the scientific, technological and artistic processes of wealth creation, poverty reduction, nation-building, and the eventual national development efforts are galvanised and attained.

As Ackers[20] stresses, "...since the 1980s, international relations have virtually been visited with barrages of successive disputes over the foundations of aspects of labour

---

[20] Ackers, P., and Adrian, W., Understanding Work and Employment: Industrial and Labour Relations in Transition, Oxford: Oxford University Press, 2003

Dror, Y., The Capacity to Govern, London: CASS, 1984

and industrial relations, which until then had been taken for granted. Thus, scholars[21] have increasingly challenged the persistent core assumptions, for instance, about the meaning of sovereignty as argued by most African countries, which oppose international interference in their labour issues, or the implications of anarchy and policies on human labour vis-à-vis the production and consumption of goods and services. Yet, another core concept has been frequently addressed in various guises and rubrics but till today has never been systematically disentangled even at the level of interdisciplinary debates such as the human labour element in international relations and in particular foreign policymaking.[22]

Essentially, be it at the national or international relations, man must work, because work is his primary economic activity; and the purposes of man's economic activity is to harness his own material conditions and economic factors of life,[23] including his dignified self-placement and relevance in his pursuit of his existentialism. Thus, man becomes dominantly different from other creatures, given his higher cognitive level in national and international affairs. In making man's labour relevant, there must exist good relations between the employer and employees. In Engels (1770 -1831) words:

[...]the failure of the man in emerging states is a function of his inability to conquer nature through his cognitive capacities, especially in utilising his atom of energy - labour with dignity in the processes of production. These cognitive capacities become the central vector in policymaking, which

---

21 Boyer, G., and Robert S., "The Neoclassical Tradition in Labor Economics." Industrial and Labor Relations Review, 54 (2), 2001, pp. 199 –223.

22 Ake, C., A Political Economy of Africa, London: Longman, 1981

23 Ibid., p.3

prod dignified labour and industrial relations practices to enhance development in societies.[24]

Thus, while in England, Engels became horrified by the disdainful character of child labour, environmental damage, low wages, bad conditions, poor health, death rates – and the 'social and political power of your oppressors'. Thus, said differently, the frameworks and channels through which industrial and labour relations is regarded as a man's dependable, necessary, inevitable and respected partner in the processes of national development are radiated by the nature of public policies for managing politics, economics through the concept of human atom of energy, otherwise called labour. Furthermore, the fashioning of an enabling or coercive character of labour - skilled or unskilled, cognitive, psychomotor or affective domains, respected or snubbed arises from the mindsets of managers of public affairs – the State, its government and people thereof.

As Williamson[25] observes, "…it is these policies that finally fashion the oddity of industrial and labour relations between the state, public or private employers of labour and the workers, at the individual or collective scale; and which finally produce exhilarating or humdrum character of societies and citizens' livelihood therein." In the believe that, labour has the capacity to overturn world hunger, poverty and sordid material conditions and economic factors a Cameroonian[26] musician sang, "*…le vrai magique ce le travail*" translated as "…true magic for wealth is work". Actually, this makes the pertinence of labour as a viable politico-social and economic-cultural instrument of development. But to the scholar of

---

24 Engels, F., The Conditions of the Working Class in England. London: ME Press, 1770 -1831

25 Williamson, O., The Economic Institutions of Capitalism, New York, Free Press, 1985

26 Kamga, J. M., Le vrai magique de l'argent ce le travail, Yaoundé : CMC, 2021

public administration, political science or sociology, the ensuing question is: What is labour and how can we, beyond rhetoric of capitalism characterise the utilisation, utility and benefits of labour, vis-à-vis the products of such labour, such as goods and services and development in societies?

3. Labour and industrial relations practices versus capitalism in postcolonial Africa's states: A brief exposition

Essentially, in a domineering posture, capitalism holds that, labour and industrial relations must be subjected to the caprices of private property, in exchange for a wage, hence, there is need to expound the concepts of labour, industrial and relations in their three operational meanings, namely: industry, labour and relations. Industry refers to any combination of efforts in the production of goods or services in which an individual or group of individuals invest financial resources. It could be a sugar industry, the beer industry, the palm oil industry, the cocoa industry, the car industry, the education industry, the insurance or banking and finance industries, and so on. By labour we refer to the human atom of energy exerted in using the objects and instruments of labour – the brain, hands, legs, knives, hoes, machines, land, and so on; to actualise the means of production. Herein, we also mean he human atom of energy to realise a specific wealth creating task. By relations, we mean "the intra and inter interactions that must exist in or between industries, especially between the employer and employee. As Kay[27] opines, "The term labour and industrial relations connotes those politico-economic and socio-cultural activities, which stem directly or indirectly from union/worker - employer relations, geared to wealth creation from which capitalism strategises to exploit

[27] Kay, G., Development and Underdevelopment: A Marxist Analysis, London: MacMillan, 1982

the workers, thereby reckoning labour as a commodity from which oppressors must garner private wealth."

Nevertheless, the separation of ownership from control within the individual firm and the role played by the state in directing and planning capitalist production, has denied L&IR much of its overwhelming significance. To claim that private property is now a historical relic of an earlier phase of capitalist production would perhaps, be to exaggerate the importance of what Galbraith[28] calls the "*techno-structure*" whereas, it is true saying that, the personal gains of the individual capitalist still remain the means through which the principle of primitive accumulation of wealth thrives as a social force against L&IR practices, especially in Africa.

Thus, the working-class struggle is not a historical constant, both in its form and content, rather it changes in response to the development of capitalism. It is not that once demands are obtained, such as eighth or ten-hour day work, free education and full employment, and so on; labour loses its significance however partial this satisfaction might be. But that the ongoing struggle of the working class for higher wages and against sordid material conditions and economic factors must themselves be changed by the development of capitalism. As the mode of production develops and capital realises itself ever more fully as a negate relation of production, working class struggle is continually transformed to wrestle the immediate and contingent forms of capitalism; wherein labour challenges the very foundations of capitalist existence. Marxists therefore opine that as the ownership of the means of production ceases to hold against labour, the centre stage of the struggle against capital is forced by the objective conditions of labour to become a struggle against primitive gathering, subjugation, alienation and exploitation.[29]

---

[28] Galbraith, J., The New Industrial State. Boston: Houghton-Mifflin, 1967

[29] Knight, F., "Laissez Faire: Pro and Con." Journal of Political Economy,

3.1. The objectives of labour and industrial relations

a) According to Kaufman,[30] certain objectives incarnate L&IR practices, namely:

b) To safeguard the interest of labour and management by securing the highest level of mutual good-will among all those within the industry, for the benefit of wealth production, social harmony and human development;

c) To avoid industrial conflict or strife by developing pleasant relations, which are an essential factor for productivity and industrial progress of a country;

d) To raise the productivity levels, during the periods of full employment, by lessening the trends of low turnover and frequent absenteeism;

e) To establish and promote the growth of an industrial democracy based on labour/management partnership in the sharing of profits and of managerial decisions, so that individual's personalities may grow its full stature for the benefit of the industry and of the country at large;

f) To eliminate or minimise strikes, lockouts and ghost towns by providing reasonable wages, improved living and working conditions, otherwise called fringe benefits;

g) To improve the economic conditions of workers and the country; and enhance national development;

h) To provide theoretical and empirical constructs, explanations, understanding and scholarship of the

75, (6), 1967, pp. 782–95

[30] Kaufman, B. E., How Labour Markets Work: Reflections on Theory and Practice by John Dunlop, Clark Kerr, Richard Lester, and Lloyd Reynolds. Lexington: Lexington Books, 1988

nexus between labour and industry; and employees, employers and the state;

i) To socialise industries by making the state itself a major guarantor of labour, with deep concerns for industrial harmony through soundly articulated public policies that enhance national cohesion.

In order to understand the theoretical and intellectual underpinnings of these concepts, Budd[31] discusses four schools of thought, namely:

(i) the Neoclassical Economics School,

(ii) the Human Resource Management School

(iii) the Industrial Relations School, and

(iv) the Critical Workplace Sanity School for dealing with what has historically been referred Labour and Industrial Relations.

Similarly, he identified three types of Labour and Industrial Relations, namely:

a) Labour relations i.e., relations between union-management (also known as labour-management-relations);

b) Group relations i.e., relations between various groups of workmen i.e., workmen, supervisors, technical persons, and so on;

c) Employer-employee relations i.e., relations between the management and employees.

All reasoning about a theory – or theories – of industrial relations has to be based on the fact that, the concept has double signification:

---

31 . Kaufman, B. E., How Labour Markets Work Op. Cit, p.36, 1988

- on the one hand, it refers to the practice which is related to the employment relationship in working life, in the labour market and in politics;
- on the other hand, it refers to the research and education activities which have this practice as their object of study.

Thus, the object of study of labour and industrial relations as a field of research and education can be defined as "the study of the employment relationship, it purposes, politics, policies, economics, social and cultural settings." This definition seems to be accepted all over in the international literature on labour and industrial relations, research, although inside this, theory problems still arise.[32] The employment relationship can be studied with the help of the theoretical and methodological tools of many social science disciplines: economics (particularly labour economics), business studies, sociology, psychology, labour law, political science, public administration, and history and economic history. The fact that almost a whole social science faculty can be mobilised in order to study the employment relationship has a great deal to say about the complexity of this discipline and the necessity of L&IR. This multi-disciplinarity may contain strong internal tensions, sometimes finding expression in shifts of centres of gravity, sometimes also demarcation battles, which can be explained by the lack of hardcore coherent theory of labour and industrial relations, similar to, for instance, neo-classical theory in economics.[33] Despite all these internal tensions, most (L&IR) scholars[34] seem to regard the following items as being related to the employment relationship, and thus are included in the field of research of labour and industrial relations.

---

[32] Ibid., p. 38
[33] Ibid., p. 45
[34] Ibid., p. 60

The interest of organisations in the labour market, their mutual relations and their relations to the state.

- The collective bargaining system at different levels; especially in the wage formation systems.
- Labour law legislation, its application and effects, particularly as regards conflict resolution, security of employment, employee rights to information and consultation or self and co-determination.
- The roles of the state as a third party concerning legislation on employee protection, incomes policy, the public employer functions and conflict resolution in the labour market.
- Wage systems and other forms of remuneration.
- Work organisation and production technology.
- The consideration of labour as an important aspect for respect and dignity of man in the workplace.

Prior to presenting the four theoretical perspectives at the middle level, however, I am going to discuss the relationship of Industrial and Labour Relations research to the two great all-embracing bodies of theory:

(i) The Dunlopian Systems Theory; and

(ii) The Related Pluralistic Theory - and Neo-Marxism.[35]

Irrefutably, the ultimate philosophy, which should inform all public policymaking approaches especially in the crafting of the theoretical roots of labour and industrial relations is the character of relationship that must exist between the state, employer, worker, goods/services and consumption. That human atom of energy, otherwise called labour, which is exerted during work activity, is naturally personified in man, and manifested through employment/work. It is thus, the

[35] Ibid., p.61

fundamental idea, which persuasively stands as the bedrock for wealth creation in societies. Goods and services are thus, the dependent variable, which become the products of labour, once labour power is exerted upon any asset - land, water, air, trees, animals, fishes, minerals and so on.[36] Nonetheless, like the other social sciences, the L&IR as a formal scholarly venture dates to the early 1920s[37] in North America, the late 1940s in the United Kingdom, and one to two decades later in other countries and regions, such as Africa and Latin America and so on.

As an identifiable area of teaching and research, its roots extend back into the nineteenth century,[38] and over this period, researchers have attempted identifying the core principle that distinguishes the subject-matter of labour and industrial relations from other labour fields, such as labour economics in order to build upon those principles or theories, which attempt to explain key labour and employment processes and outcomes. Given the insufficient literature in this domain, particularly in emerging democracies - Africa, Latin America and parts of Asia; there appears to exist great inhibitions that dwarf the offering of succinct theoretical explanations, understanding and empirical knowledge; irrespective of the fact that, the discipline of industrial and labour relations is wholesomely devoted to the important task of wealth creation for mankind; through man's economic activity of work – labour; initiated by God through Adam for man's survival in the world.[39] Given the vast intellectual lacuna in L&IR, this paper divulges the policies implications for labour and employment relations even as labour remains the substratum societal wellbing.[40] In particular, we attempt

---

[36] Ibid., p.61

[37] Ibid., p.61

[38] Wright, Patrick, Dunford, and Snell., "Human Resources and the Resource Based View of the Firm." Journal of Management, Vol. 27, No. 6, 2001, pp. 701–21

[39] The Holy Bible, KJV, p.2

discerning five contributions loaned from Hyman[41] to buttress how Africans' should think of the pragmatic application of good policies on labour and industrial relations, thus:

(i) Understanding labour's historical trends to identify the field's core theoretical and normative principle, which is that labour is embodied in human beings not as an ordinary commodity, but as a principle of human dignity.

(ii) Applying this principle to develop a theoretical explanation for the twin dependent variables of labour and industrial relations, the use of human labour to crystalise employment relationship and its attendant labour problems on the one hand; and the usage of the product of labour – goods and services, which are separated and alienated from the worker.

(iii) Development of this theoretical explanation using concepts from labour economics, the US industrial and labour relations' intellectual home base, and in so doing helping to mix original and new versions of labour needs for human progress, prosperity and happiness.

(iv) Using the identified theoretical framework as a platform for producing wide-ranging critique of neo-classical labour economics and, to a minor point, human resource management theories.

(v) As an identifiable area of teaching and research, its roots extend back into the nineteenth century,[40] and over this period, researchers have attempted identifying the core principle that distinguish the subject-matter of industrial and labour relations from other labour fields, such as labour economics and

[40] Ibid., p.2

build upon these principles or theories, which attempt to explain key labour and employment processes and outcomes.

(vi) Advancing this framework to gather new concepts and hypotheses about the work relations amid the employer and employee, including the delineations of the field's central proposition, which puts it on the scale of independent a valuable academic and professional discipline endowed unto man in society[41].

3.2. Conceptualising and contextualising the subject-matter of labour and industrial relations: An overview

The subject-matter and key structures of labour and industrial relations must first be delineated, especially as this affects the character of labour relations and wealth creation in emerging democracies in Africa. Certainly, a number of researchers and scholars[42] have defined and conceptualised labour and industrial and labour relations in Africa nevertheless much and in-depth analysis is still necessary. In this direction, two points deserve highlight as a passage to the postulations that follows.

The first is that, industrial and labour relations needs both broad and narrow acceptance in Africa. The original pre-World War II, labour and industrial relations paradigm made its core - the employment relationship and positioned itself as a critique an alternative to the labour theory of classical/neoclassical (orthodox) economics, which attempted to teach economic theories to Africans.[43] Substantially,

---

[41] Hyman, R., Industrial Relations: A Marxist Introduction. London: MacMillan, 1975

[42] Ibid., p. 34

[43] Hassan, S., The Labour Movements in Africa: A Study of the Nigerian Labour Congress, Lagos: PET, 2013

further, in the US than elsewhere, early labour and industrial relations comprised not only collective bargaining, negotiations and union studies; but also in equal measure the study of personnel/human resource management and labour and occupational law.[44] Below are some opinions drawn from scholars'[45] in the field which portend individual merits and demerits:

a) rules of the workplace (Dunlop 1958);
b) job regulation (Flanders 1965);
c) social regulation of production (Cox 1971);
d) the employment relationship as structured antagonism (Edwards 2005);
e) social regulation of market forces (Hyman 1995);
f) the process of capitalist mode of production, incarnated by peoples' labour in wealth creation efforts, but
g) the derided and skewed political and social class relations (Caire 1996);
h) conflict of interests and pluralist forms of workplace governance (Kochan 1998);
i) class mobilisation and social injustice (Kelly 1998);
j) the advancement of efficiency, equity, and voice in the employment relationship (Budd 2004);
k) collective representation and social dialogue (European Industrial Relations Observatory 2002); and
l) representation and political regulations of different interests (Eberwein, Tholen, and Schuster 2002).

44.Asobie, A. H., Labour, Manpower and the Pilferers of National Economies, Nsukka: UNN Press, 2015

45 Ibid., 35

3.3. The core principle of labour and industrial relations: Brief historical antecedents

Formal engagement into the discipline of labour and Industrial relations originated as a response to the worldwide "Labour Problem" or "Social Question" that emerged and grew in aggressively industrialising countries in the period roughly spanning 1870–1920.[46] The overarching goal of American industrial and labour relations founders was to solve this Labour Problem but within the context of a democratic capitalist economic system.

This United States' ambition was indicated in the remarks by Commons.[47] that, his life objective was, "to save capitalism by making it good", yet capitalism has been at the forefront of downgrading labour. Early labour and industrial was thus positioned as a "middle way" programme between laissez-faire capitalism and socialist revolution. The labour and industrial relations diagnosis of the Labour Problem was that, it grew out of the dysfunctional and inhumane intellectual foundations of the labour and industrial relations field.

Léon Walras established a mainstream position in his Elements of Pure Economics (1954),[48] as the natal place of neo-classical theory of general equilibrium (GE). He claims, "...the focus of economic science is that market exchange as the task for economics was to determine the laws which purchase and sell to conform spontaneously. Indicatively, as Kaufman[49] opines, "...this outcome depends critically on the assumption that, the goods or services traded are homogeneous, the property of commodities such as shares of stock and bushels of wheat." Thus, when Walras came to

46 Robbins, L., The Nature and Significance of Economic Science. London: Macmillan, 1932

47 Franck, P., Human Labour the Growth of the European Enterprise, Stockholm: Man Press, 2007

48 (1954), Elements of Pure Economics

49 Kaufman (2010:3)

factor markets, he proceeded to model labour as just one more of *N* commodities for which price and quantity are determined by demand, supply, and competitive bidding in a perfect market.

This handling of labour became standard in the practice of industrial and labour relations, which has wrongly remained so till date among many economists. Thus, the additional example from the history of thought as this concerns the usage of labour is the subject of this paper. For instance, in his famous *Managerial Dilemmas* Miller Gary,[50] asserts that, "...the general case that, the normal value of everything, whether it be a particular kind of labour or capital or anything else, rests, like the keystone of an arch, balanced in equilibrium between the contending pressures of its two opposing sides; (i) the forces of demand press on the one side, and (ii) those of supply on the other."

Consequently, as Miller and his likes believe,[51] the differences between the two are not fundamental from the point of view of theory. These examples illustrate that a commodity theory of labour and a frictionless demand and supply, and sell high syndrome of the employment relationship was at the core of early neoclassical labour economics. The theory of demand and supply as a core tenet in capitalist production system provides, in turn, an intellectual irrational rationale for a laissez-faire and unregulated regime of free trade in labour, unilateral and harsh labour management practices, with commercial money ethos that regard the output of canned fish as more valuable than the health of the children producing it, and seemingly, this suggests profanity in human material conditions.

---

50 Miller, G., Managerial Dilemmas, Cambridge, Cambridge University Press, 1991

51 Ibid., p. 78

4. Policymaking's implications for L&IR: The nexus and benefits for development

So, it is prudent considering the character of policy sequence in the historical, social, economic and labour evolutionary practices, which Schumpeter[52] labeled, "policy, economics, labour and sociology nexus." Evidently, the nexus between public policies and labour and industrial relations appears too thin and tight to be ignored in Africa's postcolonial states, which must seek to use labour power in positioning themselves in the annals of human development. Of particular interest to Africa's labour reformers, are the historical economic and social trends, which provided the theoretical threshold and support for Germany's pioneering labour and industrial relations programmes in the 1880s regarding that countries policies priority to labour issues, such as accident, unemployment, hygienic conditions, healthcare, and old age social insurance, wage levels, importance of creating solid democratic frameworks within the movements amongst other practices. These programmes were widely accepted and catapulted into the US as the opening blocks for socialist trends within the US with a core market economy in a core capitalist society.[54]

According to Rutherford[53], In the 1910s historical and social economics from German ideas procreated the American School of Institutional Economics (ASIE) and its labour subfield, the industrial and labour relations; and the strong influence of the German tradition on Wisconsin labour scholars is well illustrated in the pages of McCarthy's book, The Wisconsin Idea[54]. In it, he explained that German labour

---

52 Schumpeter, J., History of Economic Analysis. New York: Oxford University Press, 1954

53 Rutherford, M., "Institutionalism Then and Now," Journal of Economic Perspectives, (15), 2001, pp. 173–94.

54 McCarthy, C., The Wisconsin Idea. New York: Macmillan, 1912, pp. 30–31.

and industrial relations professors repeatedly came to Wisconsin and had been surprised by the entrenched German spirit in the university's labour and industrial relations department. Therefore, it is only natural that the legislation of Wisconsin should receive an impetus from men who believed that laws can be constructed as to lead to progress and at the same time preserve to the fullest of all human betterment.

Thus, the advice from scholars may be sought to the extent that, it was discovered how public policies soundly articulated based on promoting theoretical and empirical practices on labour and industrial relations had made Germany happy and prosperous, so much that, same could be catapulted and duplicated in the US or elsewhere, where the mindsets of public authorities are attuned to human development governance. In opposition to orthodox economics, Ely[55] asserts, "…labour movements and organisations are often of a great advantage to national economies, because they balance what is otherwise a "one-sided determination of the price and conditions of labour and they remove almost unlimited control of the employers over employees within defined democratic legislations," hence these movements evoke development as opposed to underdevelopment. From the foregoing analysis, this paper divulges that, labour and industrial relations properly represent:[56]

a) an independent domain of study and practice distinct from labour economics or economics; and that it covers the totality of the employment relationship.

b) it is a corpus of theory based on man's political and social conceptions of labour as the human agent; the strategic interdependence that exists between imperfect

---

[55] Ely, R., The Past and Present of Political Economy. Baltimore: Johns Hopkins University Press, 1884

[56] Edwards, P., 'The Employment Relationship and the Field of Industrial Relations." In P. Edwards, ed., Industrial Relations: Theory & Practice, 2nd (ed.), London: Blackwell, 2005, pp. 1–36

markets and competition and imperfect organisations and cooperation; the structuring and guiding role of institutional forces emanating from the state, society, history, employer and employee organisations. It is a systems perspective that organises employment relationships into discrete models and patterns;

c) a welfare function that includes not only consumers' interests and economic efficiency of organisation and the state, but also workers' interests and distinctly the social and humanistic goals, such as procedural and distributive justice for the utilisation of labour; protection of basic human rights, such as freedom from child labour, discrimination, involuntary servitude; labour mobility; freedom of association – viable trade unionism; provision of elemental democratic procedures at work (such as participation, representation, due process of law, choices and opportunities for human self-development and self-actualisation at work;

d) a discipline that welcomes abstraction, formalisation, and mathematics, but insists on empirically informed and congruent priors at strategic places; and recognition with significant parts of the employment world, which violates marginalist conditions of divisibility, incompleteness, continuity and stationarity. It is a holistic and integrative approach that draws from and endeavours to meld theories, concepts and techniques from all the disciplines that touch on the work relationship.

Table 1: 2008 - Selected African countries employment share as indicators of human growth indices

Region	Employment Share by Status	Male	Female	Total
Africa	Wage and Salaried Workers	35.4 %	18.0 %	28.4 %
	Employers	4.0 %	1.0 %	2.8 %
	Own account workers	41.3 %	38.7 %	40.2 %
	Contributing family workers	9.4 %	42.4 %	28.6 %
North Africa	**Wage and Salaried Workers**	3.5 %	39.6 %	50.0 %
	Employers	12.4 %	2.2 %	9.8 %
	Owned account workers	22.6 %	21.2 %	22.2 %
	Contributing family workers	11.5 %	37.0 %	17.9 %
Sub-Saharan Africa				
	Wage and salaried workers	30.0 %	15.2 %	23.5 %
	Employers	1.5 %	0.8 %	1.2 %
	Owned account workers	46.8 %	40.9 %	44.2 %
	Contributing family workers	21.7 %	43.1 %	31.0 %

Source: *Rüya, G, K., and Susan, H. (2011), Comparative Study of Labour and Industrials Relations in selected African Countries, Amsterdam Institute of Advanced Labour Studies, December, ILO Working Paper 116*

Generally, the tendency in Africa's labour and industrial relations is to focus on common challenges that countries face on the degree of policies responses on labour issues. Thus, to acknowledge and distinguish commonalities and peculiarities in African labour and industrial relations, it was necessary scrutinising specific country's responses that emerge out of common patterns such as shown in the table above. This, obviously, requires to examine organised labour and industrial relations practices in African countries, while acknowledging country specific national arrangements. Such an endeavour would be a valuable resource for policy makers to design own national legislations and policies that support fundamental principles of freedom of association in democratic assemblies; the effectiveness to the right to collective bargaining, raising of own union finances (check-offs) from reduction at the sources from workers' wages; and contribute to inclusive development. This provides a basis for encouraging discussions to harmonise and coordinate policies and laws in Africa. Against this context, the paper discerned that, organised labour and industrial relations in Africa face serious challenges from public policies, although there exist several opportunities and strategies that portend enabling free-thinking unbiased actors to collectively cope with changes and contribute to solving Africa's structural problems of underdevelopment.

Conclusion

Consequently, the absence of strong economic bases, occasioned by self-seeking elitist policy, accounts for the staggering postcolonial Africa's states' underdevelopment. Herein, Marxist analysis, which permitted in-depth theoretical and empirical examination of different arguments presented above, exposes how the prevailing policies shape L&IR practices, as L&IR practices shape the humdrum character of material conditions and economic factors in postcolonial Africa's states even after several decades of self-rules. In their characteristic egoism, elitist policies on labour and industrial relations practices in postcolonial Africa's states constitute severe threats, to working class which is perpetually alienated from goods/services. Thus, to reverse the status quo, we advocate policy alternative to the rational-comprehensive model, given its avalanche of democratic orientations towards labour and industrial relations. As Fehr and Armen (1999)[57] note, "the significance of L&IR to mankind must never be toyed with by any policymakers, because L&IR covers the totality of the politics, economics and management of wealth creation, while nourishing human development through sound work ethics." Consequently, soundly articulated L&IR policies eliminate conflicts and mediate all politico-economic problems and behaviours, which arise from employment relations, within a corpus of theoretical and empirical bases for human dignity and development.

[57] Fehr E., Falk A., "Wage Rigidity in a Competitive Incomplete Contract Market." Journal of Political Economy, 107, (1), 1999, pp. 106–34.

The Constitutional Protection of Prisoners Rights in Cameroon: Challenges and Way Forward

By

Patience Sone Munge

Associate Professor of Law, Department of English Law, University of Buea

and

Wabi Wilson Wakai

Department of English Law, University of Buea

Abstract

Protecting Prisoners' Rights remains a contemporary challenge in the world. States all claim to protect these rights. However, violations of the rights continue to increase despite constitutional guarantees and protection. This paper examines the constitutional rights of prisoners in Cameroon and analyses the lapses, challenges and ineffectiveness to protection. It adopts an interdisciplinary approach with the use of content analysis and interpretation of primary and secondary sources of information as well as empirical techniques like unstructured interviews. The study is underpinned by the triple pronged theory of Henry Shue whereby States must respect, protect and fulfil the rights of prisoners under ratified International Human Rights Norms. The study argues that prisoners' rights are not novel category of rights and therefore concludes that the Constitution of Cameroon protect prisoners' rights in general terms without precision. This is thought provoking when compared to Constitutions of South Africa, United States of America and India.

Key words: Prisoners' Rights, Constitution, and Protection

Introduction

Constitutional protection of human rights generally is a feature of modern democracy and good governance. This is relevant and interesting regarding the protection of persons whose liberty has been taken away by imprisonment. The world's Prisoners population stands at over 9 million[1] and one out of every 700 people in the world is in the correctional center[2]. It is for this reason that prisoners' rights are protected at both domestic and international levels. The international protection of these rights emanates from the principle that prisoners do not part with their rights when they enter the prisons[3]. The term prisoner refers to individuals who have been placed in custody by a competent judicial or legal authority, having been convicted of one or more offences and sentenced to custody, or alternatively, where a criminal case against them is being pursued but they have not yet been tried and convicted or definitively sentenced.[4]

The preamble to the 1996 constitution of Cameroon proceeds in two ways of consecrating human rights. The first being an adhesion consecration as it provides that the people of Cameroon solemnly proclaim and attach themselves to ideas and human rights as proclaimed by the Universal

---

1 Walmsley, R., *World Prison Population List,* (6th ed), International Centre for Prison Studies, 2005, p, 14.

2 Walmsley,R., "Global incarceration and prison trends", *Forum on Crime and Society*, 3 (1/2), 2003, 65-67 at 67.

3 Principle 5 of the Basic Principles for the Treatment of Prisoners adopted and proclaimed by General Assembly Resolution 45/111 of 14 December 1990. The Human Rights Committee on the rights of persons deprived of their liberty, General Comment 21, Article 10 (Forty-fourth session, (1992)

4 B.A. Garner, *Blacks Law Dictionary* (9th ed) (West: West Publishing Co, 2004) page 513

Declaration of Human Rights[5] (UDHR) 1948 and other ratified conventions on human rights[6]. Secondly, there is a list of consecration of rights and freedoms that the state is enjoined to respect and protect within the preamble. These are generally rights belonging to the first and second generations of human rights without specific reference to any group therein[7]. Article 65 of the same constitution provides on this perspective that the preamble shall be part and parcel of the constitution. This is an exception to the general rule that preambles of constitutions donot form part of the constitution.

The protection of prisoners rights in Cameroon is embeded in the Constitution[8] and the constitution remains the *grund norm* wherein other efforts to protect prisoners rights originate[9]. This constitution, for the first time in the history of Cameroon Human Rights, came up with some human rights stipulations as provided in the preamble of the constitution.[10].

---

5 Universal Declaration of Human Rights, adopted by General Assembly Resolution 217 A (III), proclaimed by the United Nations General Assembly in Paris on 10 December 1948.

6 Examples of these ratified conventions include the ICCPR 1966, ICESCR 1966, ACHPR 1986, CAT, CRC, CEDAW among others.

7 International Covenant on Civil and Political Rights, adopted by General Assembly Resolution 2200A (XXI) of 16 December 1996, entered into force 23 March 1976; International Covenant on Economic, Social and Cultural Rights, adopted and opened for signature, ratification and accession by General Assembly Resolution 2200A (XXI) of 16 December 1966, entered into force 3 January 1976

8 Law No. 2008/001 of 14 April 2008 to amend and supplement some provisions of Law No. 96/06 of 18 January 1996 to amend the constitution of 2 June 1972.

9 The constitutionalization of human rights is both ancient and recent. Ancient in that it is derived from the French Declaration of the Rights of Man and Citizens of 1789 and recent in that we witness how it grew in the 1990s. Generally, the constitution consecrates human rights and their arrangements or layout is of an infra constitutional order.

10 It provides that 'the Preamble shall form part and parcel of the

The constitution alongside other ratified international treaties all provide for the rights of persons under any form of detention. From a monist perspective and by virtue of article 45 of the same constitution, duly ratified international treaties shall following their promulgation override national laws provided the other party to the treaty apply same. Thus, the constitution and international instruments constitute part of the same law in Cameroon. In spite of the fact that prisoners' rights enjoy considerable recognition under International Law, it finds a less receptive audience in Cameroon. In line with this, the Cameroon Human Rights Commission[11] (CHRC) has consistently reported on the dehumanizing conditions of detention in Cameroon. Annual reports of this commission continue to report that prisons are old and dilapidated, overcrowded, lack food in quantity and quality, not conducive for human accommodation, lack sufficient funding and marred with the spread of communicable diseases like syphilis, malaria, HIV/AIDS, among others[12]. The end result is the violation of the rights of prisoners within the prisons. Therefore, this paper seeks to critically discuss the limits of the constitution in protecting prisoners' rights through the spectrum of judicial decisions and state obligations under international human rights law.

1. General and Specific Rights of Prisoners in Cameroon

Constitutionally, all persons shall have equal rights and obligations before the law[13]. This cardinal principle is

---

Cameroon constitution'

[11]Cameroon Human Rights Commission., Report on the State of Human Rights in Cameroon. (Yaounde: Ets Messie Printers and Publishers, 2021)

[12] Fontebo, H.N., Prison Conditions in Cameroon. The Narratives of Female Inmates. Unpublished PhD Thesis, University of South Africa, 2013; In *Turner v. Safley* [1887] 482, U.S 78.

[13]Pursuant to the principle of equality of all citizens before the law, judicial institutions function without any discrimination.

contained in the United States Constitution as in Cameroon[14]. In the case of *City of Cleburne, Texas v. Cleburne Living Center*[15], it was held that to prevail on an equal protection claim, a prisoner must prove the following two instances of discrimination: firstly, that the State treated him or her differently from others who were similarly situated; and that the difference in treatment was not rationally related to any legitimate governmental interest[16].

Furthermore, No person may be prosecuted, arrested or detained except in the cases and according to the manner determined by law[17]. This provision is also provided in the Ethiopian constitution[18] in that no Ethiopian subject may be arrested, sentenced, or imprisoned except in pursuance of the law. This provision, however, does not have clear provision on treatment of prisoners in Cameroon and Ehtiopia. As such cannot effectively protect prisoners rights to fair hearing, arrest and detention.

Similarly, the law shall ensure the right of every one to a fair hearing before the courts[19]. This is an inalienable right found in Article 10 of the UDHR, which states that "everyone

---

[14]U.S. Constitution. amendment. XIV, (1). It embodies equality of courts, fair and public hearing, by competent, independent and impartial tribunal established by law, right to compensation in cases of miscarriage of justice, and the prohibition of double jeopardy.

[15] (1985) 473 U.S. 432, 439

[16]See *Village of Willowbrook v. Olech.* (2000) 528 U.S. 562, 564; In the celebrated case of *President of the Republic of South Africa v Hugo* (1997 (4) SA 1 CC.

[17]International human rights law instruments like the UDHR, ICCPR, UNSMR, provides that where a state practices detention, it must not be arbitrary and must be on grounds established by law.

[18] Constitution of the Federal Democratic Republic of Ethiopia, Federal Negarit Gazetta, Proclamation No. 1/ 1995.

[19] In Cameroon, the right to fair hearing must be respected in all courts be it ordinary courts, or courts with special jurisdiction. This right was first exercised by God following the events that happened in the Garden of Eden between Adam and Eve.

is entitled in full equality to a fair and public hearing by an independent and impartial tribunal, in the determination of his rights and obligations and of any criminal charge against him. Further, Article 7(1)(d) of the ACHPR specifies that the individual right to have one's cause heard includes "the right to be tried within a reasonable time by an impartial court or tribunal." Contrarily in Cameroon, Prisoners in the Yaounde, Douala, Buea and Bamenda central prisons are being held beyond the statutorily defined time limits for custody without bail, constituting a clear violation of their right to have their case adjudicated 'within a reasonable time.' In *The State Prosecutor v. Ngum Ngwane*[20], the accused was arrested and detained in Mundemba. He was later transfered to the Buea Central Prison and charged with terrorism by the Military Tribunal in Buea, charges which he pleaded not guilty. He was therefore remanded in custody. Surprisingly, as of September 2021, his case has not been heard for reasons of non-composition of the court. This is a violation of the constitutional right to fair trial as provided for under the preamble of the Cameroon constitution. This systemic shortcoming is worsened by the inaction of members of the prison administration. Specifically, interviewed prisoners claim that they are indigent and, therefore, not afforded the opportunity to make phone calls, to contact or procure legal services, or even acquire transportation to their hearing. Moreover, many of the prisoners indicated that not only were they not informed of when their court date occurred, they did not even know the reason for their imprisonment[21]. In *The People of Cameroon v. Njika Florentine and 5ors*[22], the matter was dismissed based on provisions of section 3 of the CPC for violating the need for diligent and speedy prosecution as a requirement for fair hearing. Together, these procedural

---

[20]*Military Court Buea*, (2019)

[21]See also The Prosecutor v. Apane Brandon (2019) (Military Tribunal Buea).

[22] Suit No. CFIB/011c/2006.

deficiencies amount to a gross violation of the rights of prisoners to a fair hearing. In *Southern Cameroon National Congress v. Cameroon*[23], the right to a fair hearing was violated following the arrest of Southern Cameroonians who were caught and detained for a pretty long time without trial. In *R v. University of Cambridge*[24], Fortescue J. linked the concept of fair hearing to natural law and natural justice. He issued a writ of *mandamus* to the University of Cambridge requiring the institution to restore to one Dr. Bentley his degrees of Bachelor of Arts and Doctor of Divinity of which he had been deprived of by the university without a hearing.

However, access to court as a prerequisite of the right to fair hearing remains a problem to most prisoner in Cameroon.In *The People v. Justice Nyoh Wakai and 172 Ors*[25], Justice Fombe ordered the immediate release of the prisoners who were detained successively by different administrative authorities for a continuous period of four months without hearing .

A prerequisite to the fulfilment of the right to fair hearing is the need for prisoners to be prosecuted in public. However, the requirement for public trial especially in criminal cases was violated by the court of first instance Buea in *The people v. Roland Minang*[26] and that of *The People v. Sigalla Rene and co*[27]. During the hearing of these cases, access by the public was curtailed for reasons unknown to the public. Entrances to the court were all blocked by Gendarmes and the Police officers and lawyers could only access courts by presentation of professional cards. This was the view of the United Nations Human Rights Committee in *Womah Mukong v. Cameroon*[28],

---

23 (2004) AHRLR, 43.
24 (1723) 93 ER 698.
25 (1997) 1 CCLR 127-254.
26 Suit No. CFIB/13C/2012 (Unreported).
27 Suit No. CFIB/24C/2012 (Unreported).
28 Communication No. 458/1991, UN DOC.CCPR/C/51/D/458/1991.

whereby the committee held that cameroon laws inhibit the right to access courts.

Equally, every accused person is presumed innocent until found guilty during a hearing conducted in strict compliance with the rights of the defence. Upholding this cardinal principle of criminal law and constitutional rule Lonneken Stevens[29] finds that to detain a suspect is to deprive him from his liberty without having a judge establish his guilt within a fair trial. A pre-trial detainee may turn out to be innocent in the end. Therefore, when pre-trial detention is perceived to be applied too easily, too often, or too long, it is alleged that pre-trial detention practice should be more in keeping with the presumption of innocence. The presumption requires that the state treats the suspect as if he were innocent. *In CDC v. Isa Bongam*[30], the South West Court of Appeal held that the right to fair hearing is a legal principle of natural justice which holds that no one shall be condemned unheard and requires those who handle disputes between parties to act fairly in good faith, without bias and in judicial temperament. Nevertheless, this is a normative rather then a factual assumption. Ashworth[31] supports Lonneke's idea by arguing that the presumption of innocence is a moral and political principle, based on a widely shared conception of how a free society should exercise the power to punish. The relevance of this principle in the preamble of the Cameroon constitution is to protect a detainee against arbitrary and excessive state action.

---

[29] Lonneke, S., "Pre-Trial Detention: The Presumption of Innocence and Article 5 of the European Convention on Human Rights Cannot and Does Not Limit its Increasing Use". *European Journal of Crime, Criminal Law and Criminal Justice*, 2009, 17 165-180 at 167.

[30] (1997) 1CCLR, P.261

[3131] Ashworth, A., "Four Threats to the Presumption of Innocence". *International Journal of Evidence and Proof.*, 2006, 10, 249.

More over, every person has the right to life, to physical and moral integrity and to humane treatment in all circumstances. Under no circumstances shall any person be subjected to torture, to cruel, inhumane or degrading treatment[32]. As such, the practice of putting prisoners in chains when bringing them to court or as punishment for committing an offence in the prison facility is viewed as inhuman and degrading. This explains why sections 347 of the Criminal Procedure code in support of the constitutional provisions prohibits the practice by holding that prisoners who are detained shall be brought unfettered before the court. This guarantee is also protected in various international Instruments that have been incorporated into Cameroonian law by the constitution: the UN Charter Articles 55 and 56 and UDHR Article 3 each state that "everyone has the right to life, liberty and security of person."

However, the strongest protection is found in the Convention on Torture or Cruel, Inhuman or Degrading Punishment or Treatment of 1984 (CAT). Article 1(1) defines torture as: "...any act by which severe pain or suffering, whether physical or mental, is intentionally inflicted on a person for such purposes as obtaining from him or a third person information or a confession, punishing him for an act he or a third person has committed or is suspected of having committed, or intimidating or coercing him or a third person, or for any reason based on discrimination of any kind, when such pain or suffering is inflicted by or at the instigation of or with the consent or acquiescence of a public official or other person acting in an official capacity. It does not include pain or suffering arising only from, inherent in or incidental to lawful sanctions."

The state shall guarantee the child's right to education. The relevance of this right is hightened by the fact that it

---

[32] In *Conjwayo v. Minister of Justice, Legal and Parliamentary Affairs and Others* (2) SA 56, 1992

constituted one of the Millenium Development Goals (MDG) which is now Sustainable Development Goals (SDG). It provides for the universal realisation of literacy through compulsory primary or elementarry education. This however is not meant for only free citizens or those who enjoy their liberty but applies to prisoners, especially juveniles. It is a cardinal principle of international human rights law that the practice of detention must not be carried out in such a manner that it destroys the life projects of a child.

Nevertheless, eventhough Cameroon has actually achieved the right to universal education through free elementary education, it is not however compulsory as a child under prison custody does not have this chance to attend elementary education. This applies also to children who come from poor background, independent of the fact that they enjoy their liberty. Thus, the realization of the right to compulsory elementary education must be adopted in prison administration. This reform can move from informal education to formal education as the latter is practiced in the prison milieu to an extent as not all prisoners have the opportunity to participate. There are several benefits for prisoners to acquire complusory universal primary education. The resulting impact spans from realization of the SDG, awareness on health standards and care, struggle to advocate for respect and improvement of detention conditions and facilitates reintegration of the prisoner back into the society where he comes from.

These rights are general rights of Cameroonians without any distinction as to race, status, colour, nor religion or nationality and so apply to prisoners as Cameroonians. However, prisoners rights have been accorded specific recognition in constitutions of some states the world over. But this is not the case in Cameroon. In the Ecuador constitution, article 35 of the constitution provides that elderly persons, girls, children and adolescents, pregnant women, persons with disabilities, persons in prisons and those who suffer disastrous or highly complex diseases shall receive priority and specialized care in the public and private sectors. The constitutions of Egypt and Ethiopia provide for an omnibus provision requiring the preservation of the human dignity of detained persons[33]. In strong terms, the Togolese constitution[34] provides that every person who is detained shall nonetheless be treated in a manner that preserves the dignity and physical and mental well-being which shall help with his re-admittance to society. This is highly applauded as it does not only contemplate the detained persons' rights during and after trial but his or her post trial rights upon relaese. Rights that are not contemplated by the constitution of Cameroon.

Nevertheless, to add force to the rights provided in the preamble of the constitution, article 1, paragraph 3 of the same constitution upholds the need for recognition of general human rights by stating that 'the State shall ensure the equality of all citizens before the law'. This is very relevant to the protection of prisoners rights as the concept of equality and non discrimination form the backbone to enjoy and have other human rights protected.

2. Constitutional Obligations to Protect Prisoners' Rights in Cameroon

States obligations to protect prisoners' rights have been asserted by Henry Shue in his triple pronged theory[35]. He

---

[33] Article 42 of the Egyptian Constitution of 2014 and Article 21 of the Ethiopian Constitution of 1995.

[34]Article 16 of the Constitution of Togo of 1992 as amended in 2007. It provides that Every accused person or detained [person] must benefit from a treatment that preserves their dignity, their physical and mental health and that aids their social rehabilitation

[35] Shue, H., Basic Rights: Subsistence, Affluence and US Foreign Policy. Princeton: Priceton University Press, 1980; H. Shue., "Basic Rights".*Essays in Philosophy*, vol. 9, No 2, 2008, 1-8 at 6

asserted the tripartite analysis of the obligations of States under international human rights instruments. These obligations were affirmed by the Maastricht Guidelines on the Violation of economic, social and cultural rights in 1997.These guidelines represent contemporary statutes of international law.

The theory holds that States are under the obligation to respect, protect and fulfill the rights of its citizens[36]. In the context of socio-economic rights, the duty to respect entails that states should not directly infringe the rights of its citizens[37]. For instance, by failing to provide citizens with their basic necessities or means for the realization of their basic needs like food, water, education, good health and shelter amounts to a direct infringement of their rights[38]. This fits well into the context of this research as prisoners rely on the state for the enjoyment of some of their basic rights like the right to good health, right to fair hearing, the right to a good and conducive standard of living. This is equally supported by the claim that whenever a state deprives somebody of his or her liberty by imprisonment, it also deprives him or her to access outside assistance from friends, family, lawyers and doctors. Accordingly, the State assumes the role of direct and immediate guarantor of the right to life, to good health, and humane treatment for persons in state custody, given that such persons are impeded from satisfying on their own a

---

[36]The Vienna Convention on the Law of Treaties specifies that States parties are bound by their treaty obligations and all treaty obligations must be performed in good faith (the principle of *pact sunt servanda*). Article 27 of the Vienna Convention reads: "A party may not invoke the provisions of its internal law as justification for its failure to perform a treaty.

[37] Tunkin, G., *Theory of International Law*. London, 1974, p. 81.

[38]It is an obligation to abstain from taking actions that could violate the rights of detainees. This is a negative obligation that obliges states not to violate human rights and can be contrasted with the obligation to protect and fulfill which are positive obligations.

series of basic necessities that are essential for the development of a dignified life[39].

The duty to protect human rights obliges States to take all legal and institutional measures to ensure that third parties do not infringe on the rights of its citizens[40]. The State protects them both from the infringement by the States own instrumentalities and other persons within its jurisdictions. This explains why the state has enacted the Cameroon Penal Code[41] to punish those who violate the rights of citizens through criminal acts. For example, the right to life is protected by criminalizing the crime of murder and capital murder as demonstrated in sections 275[42] and 276[43] of the penal code. The right to property is protected by criminalizing theft; aggravated theft under section 318[44] and 320[45] of the

---

39Case of *Children Rehabilitation v. Paraguay* (Panchito Lopez case) 2 September 2004, series C, No.112, paras 205-206.

40Under article 1 of the African Charter, States assume the obligation to "adopt legislative or other measures to give effect" to the rights protected under that treaty.

41Law No. 2016/007 of 12 July 2016 enacting the Cameroon Penal Code.

42Whoever causes another's death shall be punished with imprisonment for life.

43Whoever commits murder : after premeditation; or by poisoning; with a view to trafficking th organs of the victim; in the preparation, facilitation or commission of a felony or misdemeanour, or to enable the escape or to procure the impunity of the offender of of an accessory to such felony or misdemeanour, shall be punished with death.

44Whoever causes loss to another: by theft, that is by removing his property; or by misappropriation that is by destruction, waste or conversion of any property capable of being removed entrusted to him for the purpose of custody, return, accounting or any particular manner of dealing; by false pretence, that is by influencing him deceitfully by tricks or by misrepresentation: shall be punished with imprisonment for from 5 to 10 years and with a fine of from 100.000 to 1.000.000FCFA.

45 The penalties provided for in section 318 above shall be doubled if the theft was committed either: with force, or bearing weapons, or by breaking in, by climbing in, or by the use of a false key, or with a motor vehicle; whoever commits a theft by the use of force causing the death of another or grievous harm as provided in section 277 and 279 of the penal code

penal code and the protection of the right to dignity and prohibition of inhuman, cruel and degrading treatment is by criminalizing the offence of assault on a person by the Penal Code[46].

The UN Covenant on Civil and Political Rights contains several provisions that have been used by the Human Rights Committee to formulate State obligations to protect prisoners against each other as well as against themselves. Especially relevant are article 6 (1), which demands that the right to life 'shall be protected by law', and article 10(1), which stipulates that 'All persons deprived of their liberty shall be treated with humanity and with respect for the inherent dignity of the human person'. In the case of *Barbato v. Uruguay*[47], the Human Rights Committee recognizes that the right to life implies that the state has a duty to take adequate measures to protect the life of a prisoner against suicide, forced suicide and killing by others while in custody. And in the case of *Daley v. Jamaica*[48] the State's neglect to take measures to protect the complainant, who was assaulted regularly by other inmates, was one of the main factors that led the Committee to conclude that article 10 (1) ICCPR had been breached.

The duty to fulfill requires that states should take positive measures towards the realization of the rights of its citizens. These measures can be administrative, financial and legislative as well as in the form of policy initiatives, monitoring and education. That is, the making available of adequate funds to the prison sector is a measure to fulfill the rights of prisoners. Fulfillment implicitly will imply the availability, accessibility, adequacy and provision of quality goods and services to citizens.

---

shall be punished with death.

[46]Section 277 of the Penal code.

[47]HRC, View of 21 October 1982, Comm. 84/1981, para 9.2 and 10(a).

[48] HRC, View of 31 July 1998, Comm. 750/1997, para 76.

Hence, the triple pronged theory provides a gate way to investigates Cameroon's engagement to respect, protect and fulfill the rights of prisoners as provided in international law. The United Nations Committee on Economic, Social and Cultural Rights has developed a number of indicators for assessing compliance with this aspect of state obligations.

In Cameroon, the International Covenant on Civil and Political Rights (ICCPR) remains the core international human rights treaty on the protection of the rights of prisoners. Cameroon has ratified the Covenant and is bound to incorporate its provisions into domestic law and state practice. The International Covenant on Economic, Social and Cultural Rights (ICESR) states that everyone should have a right for getting the highest attainable standard of physical and mental health prisoners inclusive. Also, the United Nations Standard Minimum Rules for the Treatment of Prisoners, 1955 consisting of five parts and ninety-five rules. Part one providing the rules for the general applications. It declares that there would be no discrimination on grounds of race, colour, sex, the languages, religions, political views or other opinion, national or social origin, property, birth or any other status. At the same time, it is strongly need of respecting the others' religious belief and moral precepts of the group to which the prisoners belong. The Standard Minimum Rules respects the consideration to the separation of the different categories of prisoners. It indicates that the men and women must be detained in separate institutions. The under- trial prisoners must have to keep separate from the convicted prisoners. The UN standard Minimum Rule states that, it is mandatory to provide the separate residence for young and child prisoners from the adult prisoners. Subsequent UN directives have been the Basic Principles for the Treatment of Prisoners and the Body of Principles for the Protection of All Persons under Any Form of Detention or Imprisonment.

3. The State of Prisons in Cameroon

In Cameroon, several attempts have been made to ensure the effective protection of prisoners rights. There are constitutional provisions as well as legislative enactments that protect prisoners. Inspite of this, the social reality of prisons in cameroon presents the opposite.The Cameroon Human Rights Commission has consistently reported on the dehumanizing conditions of detention in Cameroon. Annual reports of this commission continue to report that prisons are old and dilapidated, overcrowded, lack food in quantity and quality, not conducive for human accommodation, lack sufficient funding and marred with the spread of communicable diseases like syphilis, malaria, HIV/AIDS, among others[49]. For instance, even when courts issue release orders to penitentiary authorities, these orders are not executed rapidly. In *The People v. Njungwe Marcel and Ors*[50], the prisoners spent over four extra months in prison for not being able to pay 'departure dues'[51] illegally imposed by the prison authorities.

Furthermore, an important element of current incarceration practices is the concept of reformation, namely, that a prisoner should come out of prison a better person. However, if the prisoner is to be reformed for his or her eventual return into society, then it is essential that the prisoner is treated humanely during incarceration. Nevertheless, it would appear that the humane treatment of

---

[49] Fontebo.,H.N., *Prison Conditions in Cameroon. The Narratives of Female Inmates.* UnPublished PhD Thesis, University of South Africa, 2013; Cameroon National Commission on Human Rights and Freedoms., Report on the State of Human Rights in Cameroon. (Yaounde: Ets Messie Printers and Pubishers, 2017) In *Turner v. Safley*[1887] 482, U.S 78, it was held that Prison walls do not form a barrier separating prison inmates from the protections of the Constitution.

[50] Suit No. HCF/079c/2012 (Unreported)

[51] This is a sum of money given to detainees taking care of respective quarters in prisons.

prisoners in Cameroon is a luxury, with New Bell Prison Douala, a maximum security prison located in the economic capital, being classified as "hell on earth". New Bell Prison in Douala is the largest prison in the country and, yet, almost none of the basic human rights of its prisoners are respected. As regards sanitation, the septic tanks are always full beyond capacity and prisoners themselves struggle to unblock these septic tanks. The insufficient number of toilets means that some prisoners are left with diarrhoea stools on their bodies and they often go for several days without taking a bath. The situation is further aggravated by the fact that the state does not provide toiletries to prisoners as is the custom in other parts of the world[52].

In addition, because of the shortage of food some of the prisoners resort to digging in the dustbins in the prison to pick up the peelings of vegetables, cocoyams and other foodstuffs thrown away by other prisoner. This often leads to health hazards which result in the high death toll, as the state provides limited medication for the prisoners. The situation in New Bell Prison is indicative of the low levels of hygiene and insufficient food in Cameroon prisons and demonstrates the lack of care and financial commitment to prisoners and also the lack of programmes aimed at effective rehabilitation. State engagement in overcoming the problems identified above remains unsatisfactory as these problems continue to persist and is in violation of article 10 of the International Covenant on Civil and Political Rights 1966. It states that 'all persons deprived of their liberty shall at all times be treated with humanity and with respect to their inherent dignity of human person'.[53]

---

[52] A. Coyle., understanding prisons: Key issues in Policy and practice.(UK: Open University Press, 2005)

[53] The kampala declaration on similar basis provides that prisoners should retain all rights which are not expressly taken away by the fact of their detention, That prisoners should have living conditions which are

Considerable intervention by the Church and other civil society organizations is highly applauded and have been influential in the treatment of prisoners. Despite the humanitarian intervention of civil society organizations like the church[54] and other non-governmental organizations in the provision of food items, clothing, and spiritual upkeep that are relevant for the reintegration of the prisoner back into the society, such efforts have proven to be insufficient as prison conditions remain deplorable.[55] The end result is human rights violations within the prisons.

Taking accommodation for instance, the situation in the Buea and Bamenda Central Prisons has been worsened following the advent of the Anglophone crisis. The Chief of Service incharge of Discipline at the Buea central prison asserts that:

Accommodation has always been a major problem to detainees in Cameroon and this has been further complicated by the massive arrest and detention of people during the Anglophone crisis. The Buea central prison housed over 800 prisoners before the Anglophone crisis started in 2016. As of December 2018, the prison has a total population of over

---

compatible with human dignity.

54 The Church here refers to Protestant, Catholic, and other Pentecostal Churches engage in prison ministry. Both NGOs and churches work inside and outside the prison to complement the cameroonian prison service which oversight function is the rehabilitation, safe custody, and reintegration of detainees back to their communities. NGOs engage in programmes depending on their mission statemnt. They embark on educational and vocational training. Others take up specific roles in the protection of women detainees, children, and some tackle issues of overcrowding. FBO provide spiritual and physical wellbeing for detainees through group and individual counselling for reformation,change of attitude and behaviour. They equally provide food items, health care and reading materials.

55 Wabi., W.W., "Responses to Overcrowding in Cameroon Prisons: Legal and Humanitarian Perspective". *African journal of Applied Social Sciences,* Vol.10(6), 2019, 75-88:87.

1300 prisoners after the release of over 90 that benefited from the presidential pardon. A single cell now houses over 100 prisoners which is inhuman and degrading. The increase in prison population is not followed by budgetary allocations and no new cells are being constructed.[56]

Boh and Ofege[57] describe Kondengui as a prison where "prisoners wake up to line up behind each other and take turns urinating on the little mountain of faeces in one corner of the cell, chipping it off and scattering the pieces onto the floor". Tande paints a picture of Kondengui prison as a microcosm of the prison conditions in Cameroon. According to Tande, Kondengui prison is defined as "hell on earth"[58].

As regard accommodation in the Yaounde Central prison, the chief of service In-charge of socio-cultural activities states thus:

Accommodation is a major problem in the prison due to the daily increase in number of prisoners. The capacity of this prison is 1500 but as of now, the prison has 4567 prisoners comprising those awaiting trial and those that have been sentenced. This causes serious shortage of cells, beds, and other needed service. As such, some prisoners sleep out of the

---

[56] Researcher field work, Buea Central Prison, 20/12/ 2018.

[57] Boh and Ofege in H.N Fontebo., Prison Conditions in Cameroon: the narratives of female inmates.PhD Thesis, University of South Africa, 2013. P. 114.

[58] Tande, D, *An overview of Cameroon prison literature from Albert Mukong to Titus Edzoa*, 2012. Accessed online 21 January 2019; Kondengui prison was constructed for 800 people but sometimes it houses 4500 inmates. Tande describes the responses of the participants in his study thus: I was sleeping on a little bed of 40cm wide and 180cm long in a room of 4mx4 [sic]. They could say we were in the VIP quarters because we could afford our food and could arrange for our quarter to be cleaned. But, what about the others? If you go to Kondengui you would hear of Kosovo. In Kondengui prison it is possible to find approximately 1300 people in small quarters. A room that is supposed to take a maximum of 20 people will be packed with 80 inmates, with three people lying on a little bed 40 centimetres wide.

cells and on bare floor. It has led to health problems and other negative vices. This problem does not only violate prisoners' rights but poses serious security and control problems within the prison.[59]

4. Challenges to the Protection of Prisoners' Rights in Cameroon

Although international norms and standards provide that lack of resources shall not constitute a defence to a state for failing to respect, protect and fulfill the rights of its citizens, it is a major challenge that state actors in Cameroon face in the quest to protect the rights of prisoners. Lack of resources results in the shortage of human personnel needed to work either as prison staff or as human rights activists under the state. It also takes the form of limited financial resources allocated to the department of penitentiary administration. For example, the South West Regional office of the Cameroon Human Rights Commission has only 3 workers made of the branch head, a rapporteur and the secretary. This gives them a big task to make frequent visits to the prisons which are spread all over the region like in Buea Central Prison, Kumba Principal Prison, Mamfe Principal Prison, Tiko, Muyuka and Limbe. This is coupled with the fact that they have other human rights issues to attend to vis-à-vis prisoners. The end result of this is inefficiency and virtually no time to attend to other human rights issues[60].As such, instead of one staff taking care of just 5-15 inmates, the number is doubled to 30 and above. This is against the minimum rate prescribed by the UNSMRTP. In terms of financial resources, only the amount of 250FCFA is allocated

---

[59] Researcher field work Yaounde Central prison, interview of the Chief of service incharge of Sociocultural activities, 9-10th April, 2019.

[60] According to the United State Department of State, bureau of human rights and labour, country report on human rights practices in 2021, page 25.

to a prisoner daily. That notwithstanding, what gets to the prisoner is rated at 100FCFA. This amount is insignificant for human subsistence daily. The effect is that prisoners suffer from malnutrition. The reason for the limited funds allocated to the prison sector is because the protection of prisoners' rights does not form an economic priority to the state of Cameroon.

Cameroon is party to several international instruments protecting prisoners' rights both at the universal and regional levels. She has further domesticated these international norms and standards as part of her domestic laws by virtue of article 45 of the constitution. More so, human rights norms and standards have been asserted in the preamble of the constitution and the preamble as a matter of exception in Cameroon, forms part and parcel of the constitution as per article 65. However, only the 1992 decree on prison administration specifically provide for the rights of prisoners. The rest of the domestic instruments do so implicitly. As such, it was a major recommendation of the Special Rapporteur on Prisons for Africa, following her visit in Cameroon in 2002 that there is dire need of legal instruments to adequately provide for prisoners' rights[61]. It is quite the contrary situation in South Africa, Ethiopia, and Senegal where detainees' rights are constitutionally protected and implemented alongside special prison regulations.

In any sector, there are procedures to carry on day-to-day affairs. This is not an exception to state actors that are engaged in the protection of prisoners' rights. Both the department of penitentiary administration and the Human Rights Commission have administrative challenges that hinder the effective exercise of their functions in relation to

---

[61]The Ouagadougou Declaration on Accelerating Prison and Penal Reform in Africa (second pan-African Conference on Prison and Penal Reform in Africa, held in Ouagadougou, Burkina Faso from 18-20 September 2002)

prisoners. Taking the case of the CHRC, it has a duty to promote, protect and prevent torture of prisoners. This is by carrying out frequent visits to prisons and makes reports either appraising the state of human rights in Cameroon prisons. However, the commission does not have nor enjoy direct access to prisons given that they must possess a written order from the state counsel of the jurisdiction giving them the authority to inspect prison conditions. This has been a major administrative setback to the commission as most attempts to get such order have failed or taken long periods before they are issued. For few instances this commission has had to visit prisons, it has condemned the poor state of prisons in terms of accommodation, health care, feeding, sanitation and long period of detention without trial.

Lack of Political Will is a challenge that affects the treatment of prisoners. Where there is the political will, the state will definitely make resources available, especially financial resources for the improvement of prison conditions. Lack of political will by the state is equally seen in that very few policies are enacted coupled with very little discourse about ameliorating the conditions of prisoners at the domestic level. As earlier stated among the other challenges, the lack of political will is due to the fact that prisons do not form part of the Cameroon economic priority when put on the same scale with the development of the energy sector, technology, education and road infrastructure that form the basis of Cameroon anticipated emergence by 2035. This contributes to the poor implementation of the laws and amounts to Cameroon non-compliance with the triple pronged theory.

Conclusion and Recommendations

While Cameroon's protection and enforcement of prisoners' rights partly complies with international norms and standards, there is still much work that needs to be done in the protection and enforcement of these rights. It is the responsibility of the state, the courts and the relevant stakeholders to change the society's perception that prisoners have wronged the society and deserve to be punished. In other words, the courts need to remind the society that prisoners upon their release become part of the society and that it is the society that benefits when prisoners are released as rehabilitated members of the society. It is crucial that the courts and the state adhere to their obligations under international law to respect, protect and fulfill prisoners' rights without any form of discrimination as to status, race, ethnicity, nationality, language or any other factor. Though they have lost their right to liberty due to the incarceration, they are free to enjoy all other rights which they inherently possessed by virtue of their humanity. Their rights to a conducive and healthy environment, right to good food, healthcare, education as well as security should be guaranteed. This is because human rights reflect basic human needs which enhances human development. They deserve equal treatment in all domains of life as human beings.

The starting point in the protection of prisoners' rights is the incorporation of such rights in the constitution of the Republic of Cameroon. This is the practice in South Africa and she has been regarded to respect and protect prisoners' rights. This fact is supported by the manner South Africa treats prisoners in terms of accommodation, feeding, sanitation, education, health care, leisure, complaint mechanism and visits. This study therefore recommends that if Cameroon must start fulfilling her obligations to respect, protect and fulfil prisoners' rights as advocated in international human rights treaties ratified, she must copy the practice in South Africa.

Secondly, the role of the judiciary in the protection of prisoners' rights remain indispensable. As such, the empowerment of the judiciary to play its role in the proper interpretation of laws and respect of the principle of fair hearing would greatly help in the decongestion of prisons. This is feasible where in practice there is strict separation of powers among the three arms of government especially the non-interference of the executive in judicial affairs and guarantee of independence of the judiciary.

La contribution de l'avocat dans la qualité du processus décisionnel

Par

Jean Sylvain Oum

Dr/Ph. D. en Droit privé

Senior Lecturer

Université de Buea (Cameroun)

Résumé

L'Avocat camerounais a la chance d'avoir un Barreau uni, ce qui permet d'harmoniser sa déontologie. Le serment qu'il prête n'est plus seulement celui d'un simple auxiliaire de justice mais celui d'un homme de droit qui défend et protège l'homme dans tous les aspects de sa vie, le conseille, le représente, l'assiste devant les tribunaux. L'avocat camerounais fait aussi face aux nouveaux défis de l'heure qui nécessitent non seulement des changements dans la formation de l'élève-avocat, mais aussi l'obligation d'une formation continue, gage de la modernisation de la profession. Par ailleurs, les rapports avec les magistrats doivent être améliorés. L'indépendance de l'avocat doit avoir pour corollaire celui du magistrat pour assurer au mieux les droits de la défense et rendre la justice. La présente réflexion vise donc réaffirmer que les pouvoirs publics y compris le législateur doivent mettre tout en œuvre pour permettre à l'avocat de contribuer à l'œuvre de justice.

Mots clés : Avocat- Justice- Contribution-Formation- Indépendance.

Introduction

Durant l'époque coloniale, coexistaient à côté d'une justice de droit écrit, des Auxiliaires de Justice au rang desquels se trouvaient les Avocats organisés en un corps dit d'Avocats-Défenseurs près les tribunaux français du Cameroun[1].

Dès le lendemain de l'Etat fédéral, les pouvoirs publics se sont préoccupés de la profession d'Avocat au Cameroun Occidental par l'élaboration de la loi fédérale n°37 du 5 novembre 1963 portant profession d'Avocat.

Mais il a fallu attendre 1972 avec le retour au pays des camerounais formés à l'étranger, pour voir les pouvoirs publics se préoccuper non seulement de la nécessité d'une structure d'accueil de la jeunesse du pays attirée par cette noble profession[2], mais également de l'Organisation plus moderne de la profession. Ainsi naquit l'Ordre des Avocats au Barreau du Cameroun, création de la loi n°72-LF-5 du 23 Mai 1972 portant organisation de la profession d'Avocat.

De nos jours, les avocats ont conquis la société, il existe rarement de conférence sans avocats, ou de débats télévisés quelle que soit la nature sans avocats. L'avocat semble incarner à notre époque, une prééminence sociale certaine. En

---

[1] Il s'agissait par rapport à la Métropole d'une création particulière qui ne trouvait son modèle qu'en Alsace-Lorraine, où l'Avocat cumulait à la fois les fonctions d'Avocat et celles d'Avoué ; ainsi en même temps qu'il assistait ses clients et plaidait en défense de leurs intérêts, il lui était reconnu le droit de postulation et de représentation. L'expérience a montré que qu'il s'agissait d'un système d'avant-garde qui allait servir de modèle à l'ancienne Métropole lorsqu'il s'est agi de la réforme de la profession d'Avocat en France[1].

[2] BLACK, Y., « chroniques d'un retour au pays natal », *in Mon itinéraire à cœur ouvert*, L'Harmattan, 2021 p.21

politique c'est incontestable. Sur le plan de la pensée juridique et de la défense des citoyens c'est une évidence.

Pourtant, l'imagerie populaire a toujours représenté l'avocat comme étant « l'homme de la parole » qui plaide à la barre pour la défense des intérêts de son client[3]. Cette image est très incomplète. L'avocat est aussi un homme de cabinet qui reçoit ses clients, leur donne des consultations, négocie des contrats, étudie les dossiers dont il a la charge et prépare la procédure au nom et pour le compte de son client.

Curieusement, le terme Avocat n'a été défini ni par la loi organique[4] ni par le règlement intérieur[5]. Le vocabulaire juridique le définit comme un auxiliaire de justice, qui fait profession de donner des consultations, rédiger des actes et défendre devant les juridictions, les intérêts de ceux qui lui confient leur cause, et dont la mission comprend l'assistance (conseil, actes, plaidoiries) et/ou la représentation (postulation devant les juridictions où son intermédiaire est obligatoire)[6].

Il faut d'ores et déjà relever que pour les avocats l'idée de la qualité n'est pas neuve. En effet, les Ordres professionnels des avocats ont initialement interdit la publicité personnelle[7], avant que cette interdiction ne soit entérinée par la loi[8]. La

---

[3] PERROT, R., *Institutions judiciaires*, 10e édition Montchrestien, n°406, 2002, p.324

[4] Loi n°90/059 du 19 Décembre 1990 portant organisation de la profession d'avocat au Cameroun.

[5] Règlement intérieur du Barreau du Cameroun adopté par l'assemblée générale du 30 Novembre 2002.

[6] CORNU, G.,(S.dir), *Le vocabulaire juridique*, 10e édition PUF, p.114.

[7]BENICHOU, M., « La formation de l'avocat et la qualité des décisions de justice, *In* la qualité de la justice Actes du Colloque organisé les 8 et 9 mars 2007 par la Faculté de droit et des sciences politiques de Poitiers (Institut de droit public) p.107.

[8]L'article 62.1 du Règlement Intérieur des Avocats adopté le 30 Novembre 2002 fixe le cadre déontologique de la publicité, plus libéral qu'auparavant, mais toujours limité par le nécessaire respect des principes essentiels. Il

notion de qualité à proprement parlé n'a fait son apparition dans le domaine de la justice que vers la fin des années 1990[9]. Elle est défini dans le dictionnaire Larousse comme l'« ensemble des caractères, des propriétés qui font que quelque chose correspond bien ou mal à sa nature, à ce qu'on attend ».

Si la notion de qualité est récente, les décisions de justice sont depuis longtemps soumises à un contrôle. En s'inspirant des travaux de la Commission Européenne pour l'Efficacité de la Justice (CEPEJ), on retient que la qualité de la justice passe notamment par l'existence au profit du justiciable d'une défense assurée par un professionnel formé, compètent, disponible, offrant des garanties déontologiques et travaillant pour un coût raisonnable[10].

L'avocat joue un rôle non négligeable dans la qualité de la décision de justice : il formalise les demandes, développe un argumentaire et rédige les conclusions qui vont permettre au juge de rendre sa décision. On pourrait donc considérer que le rôle de l'avocat est essentiel à la qualité des décisions, dans la mesure où c'est lui qui apporte la matière à partir de laquelle la décision est rédigée[11]. Ce qui a fait dire à Olivier Laurent,

---

exige ainsi que la publicité permise à l'avocat procure une information au public et que sa mise en œuvre respecte les principes essentiels de la profession auxquels l'avocat est soumis.

[9] VAUCHEZ, A., « Les jauges du juge. La justice aux prises avec la construction de sa légitimité », in Pascal MBONGO (dir.), *La qualité des décisions de justice*, Strasbourg : Editions du Conseil de l'Europe, 2007, p.60 in Hélène COLOMBET, Alice GOUTTEFANGEAS, La qualité des décisions de justice. Quels critères ? Éditions juridiques associées « Droit et Société »2013/1 n°83/p 156 https://www.cairn.info/revue-droit-et-société1-2013-16page-155.htm. Consulté le 03.07/2021 à 14h41.

[10] Conseil de l'Europe, Systèmes judiciaires européens efficacité et qualité de la justice. Les Études de la CEPEJ N°20, édition 2014 page 171 n°3.5.

[11] COLOMBET,H., GOUTTEFANGEAS, A., « La qualité des décisions de justice. Quels critères ? Éditions juridiques associées « Droit et Société »2013/1 n°83/p 161 https://www.cairn.info/revue-droit-et-société1-2013-16page-155.htm. Consulté le 03.07/2021 à 14h41.

directeur de l'ENM[12] en août 2016 : « Il n'est pas de justice de qualité sans avocat de qualité capable de traduire en termes juridiques les intérêts du justiciable, capable aussi d'être l'interprète de ses tourments, souvent de sa souffrance, face à une institution complexe, au fonctionnement parfois peu compréhensible.[13] »

Aussi séduisant que soient ces raisonnements, il serait excessif de prime abord, en raison du principe de l'indépendance du juge, d'affirmer que l'avocat a une influence certaine sur la qualité de la rédaction de la décision ou sa motivation. Par contre, participant à la garantie du contradictoire ou de l'impartialité, l'avocat exerce plutôt une certaine influence sur la qualité du processus judiciaire voire à l'élaboration d'une décision de justice[14]. Se pose donc la question de savoir quelle influence les avocats exercent sur la qualité du processus décisionnel conduisant à la décision de justice ? Ou plus précisément, quel est le rôle de l'avocat dans l'œuvre de la justice ?

A cette question on oppose deux thèses dans l'analyse du processus décisionnel. La première est réaliste. Elle fait référence à un courant doctrinal qui eut son heure de gloire au début des années 1930 aux Etats-Unis[15]. Elle équivaut à considérer que les juges sont des êtres sociaux. Ils vivent au

---

12 École Nationale de Magistrature, unique établissement en France qui forme les magistrats du siège et du parquet, les magistrats en exercice ainsi que des magistrats étrangers.

13 DUPOND-MORETTI, E., et DURAND-SOUFFLAND, S., *Directs du droit*, Michel Lafon, 2017, p.34

14 YONDO, B., « Le combat pour un Barreau responsable maitre de son tableau » : *In Mon itinéraire à cœur ouvert*, L'Harmattan, 2021, p.50.

15 Ces juristes, souvent très différents les uns des autres, avaient en commun d'accepter plusieurs postulats méthodologiques (une observation du droit objective, scientifique, factuelle et critique; une approche descriptive et non normative) et théoriques (le droit est créé par les juges; il constitue un moyen pour atteindre certaines fins sociales; son évaluation doit se faire au regard des effets sociaux).

sein d'une communauté d'individus qui, indépendamment de la loi qu'elle s'est donnée, se structure aussi autour des normes, de valeurs et sensibilités susceptibles d'évoluer[16]. Les juges ne sont donc pas des êtres éthérés. La seconde est qualifiée de formaliste selon laquelle les juges appliquent les règles à des faits de façon à la fois délibérative, logique et mécanique de telle sorte que la décision judiciaire se réduit à un syllogisme[17]. Elle a été résumée par cette célèbre métaphore de Montesquieu décrivant les juges comme la « bouche qui prononce les paroles de la loi, des êtres inanimés, qui n'en peuvent modérer ni la force ni la rigueur[18]. »

Le droit camerounais a une dimension plutôt formaliste que réaliste au regard du serment prêté par les magistrats qui consiste à rendre les décisions conformément aux lois, règlements et coutumes du peuple camerounais. Il faut dire que la problématique ne manque pas d'intérêt pour la simple raison que la libéralisation de l'économie ainsi que les vastes chantiers en cours au Cameroun font naître des questions nouvelles et complexes, mais génèrent aussi un besoin de juristes compétents beaucoup plus important. Dans la pratique judiciaire, il faut relever les interférences que subissent aujourd'hui les décisions judiciaires au Cameroun (marchandage des décisions de justice, décisions rendues sur instructions ainsi que le mariage polémique entre le politique et l'appareil judiciaire). Sur le plan juridique la question de l'homogénéité des professions judiciaires se pose avec acuité

---

16 Philippe, A., *La fabrique des jugements*, La Découverte, 2022, p. 13.

17 Bix, B., Jurisprudence : Theory and context, Sweet and Maxwell Ltd., 4e éd., 1996,p.183 qui décrit la conception formaliste du jugement comme "un passage presque mécanique, syllogistique des prémisses vers une conclusion incontestable », In Pierre BRUNET, « Analyse réaliste du jugement juridique » Cahiers philosophiques n°147/ 4e trimestre 2016, p.11 https://www.cairn.info/revue-cahiers-philosophiques1-2016-4-page-9 htm consulté le 13/07/2021 à 19 heures.

18 Montesquieu, *De l'esprit des lois*, livre XI, chap.6, 1748.

pour réduire au maximum les conflits entre magistrats et avocats[19].

Même si l'actualité juridique ou politique peut aujourd'hui tendre à minimiser la place de l'avocat dans le processus décisionnel, il n'en demeure pas moins qu'il a une contribution certaine dans la qualité des décisions de justice rendues. Après analyse des textes, et à l'observation des pratiques du milieu judiciaire camerounais, on relève une contribution indirecte bien qu'inachevée en amont (I), et une contribution directe qui reste à parfaire en aval (II).

1. La contribution indirecte inachevee de l'avocat au processus decisionnel

Il s'agit ici d'analyser dans quelle mesure les modes de formation et de recrutement pèsent sur les relations entre magistrats et avocats. Il faut dire que la préoccupation des membres fondateurs du Barreau camerounais a toujours été d'offrir à l'avocat une formation sinon supérieure, du moins égale à celle du magistrat[20]. Mais cet objectif ne semble pas atteint car la formation initiale de l'avocat reste empirique, uniquement tournée vers le judiciaire tandis que la formation continue est n'est pas organisée.

1.1. Une Formation initiale empirique

La formation de l'avocat camerounais est purement empirique. Après les études en faculté, un stage dans un cabinet d'avocat constitue l'essentiel de la seule préparation

[19] Voir résolution du Conseil de l'Ordre des Avocats au Barreau du Cameroun n°008/2020 du 21 novembre 2020 sur la persécution des avocats au Barreau du Cameroun portant (entre autres résolutions) suspension du port de la robe pour tous les avocats, à la suite de l'arrestation et de la détention des avocats TAMFU NGARKA Tristel Richard et TCHUENMEGNE KENMEGNE Armel, poursuivis pour outrage à magistrat.

[20] YONDO, B., *Mon itinéraire à cœur ouvert*, L'Harmattan, 2021 p 52.

permettant à un jeune avocat de se lancer dans la vie professionnelle. C'est ce qui ressort de la loi n° 90/059 du 19 Décembre 1990 portant organisation de la profession d'avocat et du décret n°91/305 du 04 Juillet 1991 portant organisation de l'examen d'aptitude au stage d'avocat. Ces textes établissent les conditions de compétence juridique de l'avocat ainsi que le stage.

1.1.1. Les conditions de stage

Pour être admis à présenter un examen de stage les candidats doivent avoir étudié le droit à l'université. C'est la raison pour laquelle l'article 3 du décret n°91/305 du 04 Juillet 1991 portant organisation de l'examen d'aptitude au stage d'avocat exige la présentation d'une licence en droit[21]. Cependant, cette condition n'est pas stricte puisqu'un diplôme équivalent est aussi admis, ce qui induit un diplôme universitaire dans une autre discipline. A l'opposé, le candidat à la magistrature doit avoir obtenu un master (maitrise) en droit. Même si de nos jours la majorité des avocats disposent d'une maitrise en droit, il faut relever que l'accès à la profession d'avocat semble être au rabais. En effet, le jeune avocat titulaire d'un diplôme de licence, se trouve confronté aux affaires dont la résolution nécessite des connaissances universitaires acquises au niveau du master I[22].

En dépit de cet écueil, il faut souligner qu'après avoir été admis en stage, les avocats stagiaires sont inscrits sur la liste du Stage, à leur rang d'ancienneté fixé à la date de leur prestation de serment. Le stage à une durée obligatoire de deux ans[23]. Le stagiaire doit être à plein temps et en immersion

---

[21] L'examen national d'entrée en stage est instauré depuis le décret n°91/305 du 04 Juillet 1991.

[22] Droit de la banque, des assurances, recouvrement des créances, droit des transports et logistique, droit fiscal, droit public des affaires etc….

[23] Le stage est sanctionné par un certificat d'aptitude à la profession d'avocat délivré après admission à un examen probatoire dont les modalités sont fixées par décret.

totale dans un cabinet d'avocat[24]. Ce stage doit permettre au futur avocat d'acquérir les compétences professionnelles nécessaires au plein exercice du métier d'avocat. A cet effet, un véritable transfert de compétence doit avoir lieu. Pendant ce stage, les obligations de l'élève stagiaire sont particulièrement définies par les articles 11 de la loi du 19 Décembre 1990 portant organisation de la profession d'avocat et 20 du Règlement Intérieur.

Pendant la durée du stage, l'élève doit effectuer le travail qui lui est confié par son maître de stage. Le maître de stage doit encadrer l'élève et assurer sa formation professionnelle. Il doit l'encourager, le conseiller et lui apporter la compétence nécessaire à la pratique de la profession d'avocat. Tous les avocats inscrits au tableau ayant prêté serment depuis plus de quatre ans peuvent être maître de stage.

Cette formation qualifiée d'artisanale et familiale ne cesse de se perpétuer pourtant, les cabinets d'avocats au Cameroun ne sont pas spécialisés. Il est dès lors évident qu'un avocat ne peut plus chez un seul confrère apprendre la totalité du savoir dont il a besoin. Dans certains cabinets, le jeune stagiaire dès son arrivée est utile non pas en étudiant les dossiers ou en s'instruisant par l'étude des questions de droit, mais simplement en courant d'un appel des causes à une simple assistance dans les unités de police et de gendarmerie, ce qui peut compromettre le véritable caractère de formation de sa collaboration en qualité de stagiaire.

C'est le cas de relever que cette formation ne semble pas satisfaisante si l'on s'inspire des auteurs comme Camus qui, dans ses *lettres sur la profession d'avocat*[25] avait prévu, pour une formation suffisante de l'avocat deux années de travail chez le

---

[24] La conférence de stage est prévue par l'article 18 du règlement intérieur, complète cette formation. Elle est présidée par le bâtonnier et traite principalement des questions de déontologie mais d'autres sujets y sont abordés.

[25] CAMUS, A.G., *Lettre sur la profession d'avocat,* tome 1, 1740-1804 2e lettre.

procureur, puis trois années chez un avocat et il a prescrit un minimum de 12 à 13 heures de travail par jour.

Sans pour autant chercher à suivre scrupuleusement les conseils de Camus, il serait souhaitable afin de faire de l'avocat un véritable artisan de la justice, instaurer un tronc commun de formation. La formalisation des stages interprofessionnels permettrait de favoriser une meilleure connaissance réciproque des différents milieux professionnels. Dans ce sens, on ajouterait l'instauration de stages des auditeurs de justice en cabinets d'avocats pour une durée minimale[26] et réciproquement l'aménagement des stages en juridiction pour les avocats stagiaires. Il convient de préciser que ce cursus de formation est prévu dans les Law School ou *inns of courts*[27] si bien qu'un ancien membre du conseil de l'ordre des Avocats au Barreau du Cameroun formulait ainsi le vœu de la création des instituts de formation aux professions judiciaires[28] attendus depuis des lustres. Ce qui aurait le mérite d'allier la formation théorique à la pratique.

1.1.2. Les conditions de compétence juridique

Il convient de relever que le magistrat ou l'enseignant de droit qui entre dans la profession via la passerelle offerte par la loi reçoit une certaine formation tandis que l'avocat formé et inscrit dans un autre barreau, qui viendra exercer au Cameroun, en aura une différente. Tout laisse donc à penser,

---

26 C'est le Cas en France où l'article 3 de la loi du 05 mars 2007 relative au recrutement, à la formation et la responsabilité des magistrats prévoit que les auditeurs de justice effectuent durant leur trente-un mois de formation à l'Ecole Nationale de Magistrature un stage de six mois dans un cabinet d'avocat.

27 Maxwell-Fyfe, D., *The Inns of Court and the Impact on the Legal Profession in England*, 4Sw L.J391, 1950, https://scholar.smu.edu/smulr/vol4/iss4/2. Lu le 24/04/2022 à 19h38.

28 SOUOP, S., Plaidoiries du représentant du Bâtonnier sur le thème : relation avocat magistrats, audience solennelle de prestation de serment des avocats stagiaires du Tribunal de Grande Instance de l'Océan Kribi.

au regard de l'absence de cohérence dans l'apprentissage de la profession, qu'un avocat n'en vaut pas un autre.

En effet, par leur parcours ou leur activité, certains postulants sus désignés ont acquis une expérience professionnelle dans le domaine juridique dont la loi estime qu'elle constitue un bagage suffisant pour leur permettre d'être dispensé de la condition de stage et du CAPA. Peuvent ainsi justifier de la dispense au titre de l'expérience professionnelle au sens de l'article 8 de la loi organique, les anciens magistrats ayant accompli dix ans de service es qualité à condition cependant de répondre à la condition de diplôme. De même, en raison de leurs connaissances, les anciens professeurs, maîtres de conférences ou chargés de cours, mais à condition qu'ils aient accomplis dix ans de service *es* qualité et qu'ils aient accomplis une période de recyclage de six mois non renouvelables à la diligence du Bâtonnier, nonobstant la valeur de leur expertise dans le domaine juridique.

Sont également dispensés de stage, les avocats de nationalité camerounaise inscrits dans un barreau étranger s'ils n'ont pas été radiés du tableau, ainsi que les avocats stagiaires titulaires du certificat de fin de stage obtenu dans un pays étranger après une durée d'au moins deux années. Reste donc à savoir si la formation continue est de nature à offrir une solution satisfaisante au nivellement des connaissances entre avocats.

1.2. Une Formation continue déficitaire

Il est indispensable que, entre autres qualités, l'avocat possède un haut degré de compétence[29]. Celui-ci n'est cependant pas acquis une fois pour toutes au sortir des études universitaires ou de la période de stage. Confronté à des législations en constante évolution, l'avocat se doit tout au

[29] L'article 21 du Règlement intérieur du Barreau du Cameroun considère comme faute disciplinaire toute erreur professionnelle grave.

long de sa carrière professionnelle, d'entretenir son savoir, de le développer, de le mettre sans cesse à jour, de l'ouvrir aux matières nouvelles. Pourtant, la formation continue de l'avocat n'est pas obligatoire pour tous les avocats inscrits au Barreau du Cameroun. Cette formation est facultative et essentiellement dispensée au sein des colloques ou conférences à caractère juridique dont les modalités et le déroulement ne sont pas clairement définis.

1.2.1. Les modalités des colloques ou conférences à caractère juridique

La participation à des colloques ou conférences à caractère juridique peut être prise en compte au titre de la formation continue. Ces colloques et conférences ont généralement un lien avec l'activité professionnelle des avocats camerounais. Toutefois, aucun texte ne précise les conditions dans lesquelles ces colloques ou conférences doivent se dérouler. Ces colloques ou conférences sont organisés par le Barreau[30] ou les institutions judiciaires, ou alors par les organismes dispensateur de formation professionnelle comme le CIFAF[31], ainsi que des initiatives d'associations diverses ou personnelles des avocats sans avoir l'obligation de communiquer à l'avance au Barreau le programme détaillé de la date du colloque, sa durée, les thèmes traités, les noms et références professionnelles des intervenants, les effectifs minimum et maximum de chaque colloque et conférence, la description des supports pédagogiques diffusés.

1.2.2. Le déroulement des colloques et conférences

Il faut relever que chaque colloque ou conférence ne donne pas systématiquement lieu à la remise à chaque

[30] A la rentrée solennelle du Barreau, séminaire organisé par le ministère de la justice du 5 au 7 juin 2019 avec pour thème « Les nouveaux marchés du droit ».

[31] Centre International de Formation en Afrique des Avocats Francophones.

participant d'une documentation écrite. Il est toutefois remis, à chaque participant, par l'organisme organisateur, une attestation de présence sans qu'on ne sache selon quelles modalités la formation a été effectuée. Si cette attestation est signée et remise à l'avocat, elle ne produit aucun effet puisqu'aucune obligation n'impose à l'avocat camerounais de la transmettre au conseil de l'ordre. Elle ne servira qu'à décorer les murs des cabinets d'avocats bénéficiaires de la formation.

Aucune obligation de déclaration de sa formation continue au cours d'une année au Bâtonnier n'est exigée. Cette formation continue, même si elle a été accomplie, n'est pas assujettie au contrôle du conseil de l'Ordre. Cet organe devrait pourtant vérifier si les critères des formations suivies sont respectés, mais également que cette formation a un lien avec l'activité de l'avocat.

Le droit camerounais subit de plus en plus de nos jours des reformes avec des textes communautaires, internationaux et nationaux. La formation continue doit être prise au sérieux, parce que la qualité des décisions rendues est tributaire du niveau d'appropriation du droit par les différents acteurs.

Un frein important au développement d'une profession juridique compétente est le sentiment répandu et persistant parmi les avocats camerounais que les procès ne se gagnent qu'accessoirement sur des arguments juridiques, et que seules comptent les relations personnelles. L'avocat camerounais pense pouvoir avant tout offrir des relations avec le juge[32] (ou

---

[32] Dans un courrier adressé au Chef de l'État Camerounais et publié sur les réseaux sociaux dans une affaire opposant le Ministère Public et la Société CANA BOIS contre NGO'O Cyrus, DG Port Autonome de Douala, un magistrat du Tribunal de Première Instance de Douala Bonanjo se plaignait que les échanges WhatsApp fraternels entre lui et l'avocat de l'une parties aient été transcrits sur un procès-verbal d'huissier pour le salir et le jeter en pâture. L'avocat était constitué pour l'une des parties. Cette affaire a mis en lumière les relations obscures pouvant exister

avec tout autre personnage officiel susceptible d'influer sur le résultat du procès), cultivées sur le long terme par de fréquents présents ou invitations. Ce qui est de toute évidence de la corruption.

2. La contribution directe perfectible de l'avocat au processus decisionnel

L'avocat a une double mission à la fois juridique et judiciaire[33]. La mission juridique relève en dehors de tout procès, de la vie des affaires et la gestion des patrimoines (constitution de société, gestion immobilière, négociation, opérations contractuelles en général, etc.) tandis que le volet judiciaire de sa mission concerne ce qui a lieu en justice, ce qui suppose une procédure, une intervention dans la justice. En clair, les actes judiciaires sont ceux qui se rapportent à la justice et qui conduisent l'avocat à obtenir pour le compte de son client, une décision rendue par un organe juridictionnel. Les activités juridiques quant à elles reposent sur la consultation, le conseil[34] et la rédaction des actes[35], on verra que le champ professionnel de l'avocat s'est élargi sur ce point incorporant de nouvelles missions (médiateur, arbitre etc.) qui font de l'avocat une partie intégrante de l'œuvre même de la justice. L'avocat contribue en cela directement au processus décisionnel tant dans le cadre des activités judiciaires que juridiques.

---

entre un juge et un avocat dans le cadre d'un procès. Voir, journal Repères du 1er Juin 2022.

33 DOSSA, R., « le rôle de l'avocat dans la cité : du juridique au judiciaire », In : Revue de L'*Ersuma* n° Spécial Nov-Déc 2011. www.revue.ersuma.org consulté le 05 Mai 2022 à 17h 38.

34 Voir article 1er loi Organique et article 75 du Règlement Intérieur.

35 Voir articles 35 et suivants du Règlement Intérieur.

2.1. Dans la cadre des activités judiciaires

Dans le cadre des activités judiciaires le constat est clair, la justice camerounaise fait face à la complexification des rapports entre les juges et les avocats découlant de l'hétérogénéité de leur formation. Il serait souhaitable, afin que l'avocat participe de manière plus prégnante à la justice, que les rapports soient homogènes.

2.1.1. Les obstacles aux rapports harmonieux entre magistrats et avocats en matière de défense

Le défenseur doit dire tout ce qu'il estime utile à la défense dont il a la charge, dans la limite des lois et des convenances. En abordant un dossier en vue d'un procès, d'une audience, un magistrat peut avoir des impressions qui, si elles viennent à guider ses décisions peuvent faire des dégâts irréparables, ruiner des vies, et ternir l'image de l'institution judiciaire[36]. Heureusement grâce à la plaidoirie de l'avocat[37], ces préjugés finissent par voler en éclat par la puissance de l'audience.

Il faut dire que certains avocats croient encore à l'Etat de droit au Cameroun, ils s'efforcent à plaider et à aider le justiciable dans sa défense en justice en présentant des explications orales ou écrites en son nom. Il existe aussi au Cameroun de grands juges (même si le troupeau est petit), qui sont indépendants et impartiaux dans leur prise de décision,

[36] BADR, Y., « Souvenirs d'assises », In : Robert SALIS *Rendre la justice*, Calmann Levy, p.56

[37] La plaidoirie est l'exposé oral et le développement verbal des prétentions des justiciables, la discussion des moyens adverses et des objections légales, le développement des arguments justificatifs d'un plaignant ou d'un mis en examen. Ce sens du mot « plaider » en tant que soutenir de vive voix devant les juges les causes des parties, est un sens récent dans la langue française.

L'avocat plaidant est protégé contre une action en diffamation, injure ou outrage. Les discours prononcés ou les écrits devant les tribunaux ne donneront lieu à aucune action en diffamation, injure ou outrage. Cela s'applique aux paroles prononcées ou aux écrits produits par un avocat au cours de sa plaidoirie.

mais ont conscience de leur dépendance vis-à-vis des avocats, notamment de leurs conclusions et production de pièces, parce que rendre justice n'est pas une entreprise individuelle mais procède d'interdépendances particulières. C'est le « théorème de Truche »[38]. La justice devient ainsi une œuvre collective à laquelle participent les avocats. Malheureusement, il y a des situations de frustration où l'avocat n'a pas du tout l'impression de participer au processus de décision judiciaire.

En effet, l'avocat camerounais a toujours en face de lui des magistrats qui ne sont guère protégés contre d'éventuelles interférences extérieures dans l'exercice de leurs fonctions[39]. Ils sont nommés par le pouvoir exécutif qui les évalue et peut, le cas échéant les sanctionner[40]. Ce qui pose le problème réel de leur indépendance. Certains magistrats cherchent à se protéger en impliquant des tiers (les personnalités politiques ou judiciaires) dans leur processus décisionnel. La corruption des magistrats est aussi un problème très sérieux au Cameroun. Bien que l'ampleur de ce type de phénomène soit par définition difficile à mesurer, il ne semble faire aucun doute que de très nombreux magistrats sont corrompus. Il

---

38 ZUCHOWICZ, L., « Le théorème de Truche : réflexion sur l'in (ter) dépendance du magistrat » *In* : Robert SALIS (s.dir) *Rendre la justice* Calmann Levy, 2021, p.545.

39 YONDO, B., « Affaire Me Lydienne YEN EYOUM c/L'ETAT DU CAMEROUN & LA SGBC » *In* : *Mon itinéraire à cœur ouvert mémoires*, L'Harmattan, 2021, L'auteur reproduit à la page 117 un courrier portant ordre du pouvoir exécutif au pouvoir judiciaire de la manière suivante « j'ai l'honneur de vous notifier l'accord du Chef de l'État à vos « propositions tendant à faire déférer Mes YEN EYOUM Lydienne, BALENG MAAH, Polycarpe ABAH ABAH, Henri ENGOULOU et NGWEM au parquet du Tribunal de Grande Instance du MFOUNDI en vue de l'ouverture d'une information judiciaire contre eux, avec mandat de détention provisoire, du chef de détournement de deniers publics et complicité. Vous voudrez bien me faire connaitre, pour la très haute information du Chef de l'État, l'exécution de ses diligences ».

40 Voir art 21 et s de la loi n°82-014 du 26 novembre 1982 fixant l'organisation et le fonctionnement du Conseil Supérieur de la Magistrature.

suffit de s'en tenir aux rapports des organismes chargés de la lutte contre la corruption et sur les mesures disciplinaires prises à l'encontre des juges pour se persuader de la réalité du phénomène[41].

Au-delà du problème moral que pose la corruption, les conséquences du phénomène sont importantes. Il contribue tout d'abord au développement d'un certain mépris du juge, celui-ci étant perçu par les avocats et par les parties comme un bureaucrate corrompu[42]. Il freine le développement de l'idée de l'importance du droit dans la mentalité camerounaise. En effet, si une affaire se gagne en raison de ses relations ou de ses moyens financiers comment prendre le droit au sérieux ? Pour la même raison pourquoi les avocats investiraient-ils dans la technique du droit ?

Il faut par ailleurs déplorer que nonobstant l'implication des avocats dans la défense de leurs clients, les magistrats perdent souvent de vue que la justice est organisée pour faire du droit et non pas de la morale. Dans des affaires récentes concernant, Njeuken Loic (connue sous le nom de « Shakiro »), Mouthe Roland (connue sous le nom de « Patricia ») et Martin Camus Mimb, des juges ont voulu à tout prix transformer en scandale judiciaire des comportements

---

[41] Le rapport CONAC (Commission Nationale de Lutte Anti-Corruption) publié le 23 Septembre 2021 a établi un quinté des secteurs les plus corrompus au Cameroun en 2020, il en ressort que le secteur de la justice occupe la 5e place avec 11,30% du taux de dénonciation.

[42] Une déclaration solennelle des anciens Bâtonniers de l'Ordre des avocats au Barreau du Cameroun publiée dans les journaux relevait que « La Conférence des anciens Bâtonniers appelle solennellement les pouvoirs publics, et plus spécifiquement le Ministre de la justice, à prendre les dispositions nécessaires pour mettre promptement un terreau mépris ainsi affiché à l'égard des Avocats lequel mépris a gangréné fortement les Palais de justice de la République dans lesquels l'avocat n'a plus sa place auprès des Magistrats, ceux-ci préférant traiter directement avec les justiciables, et leur accordant plus de considération en fonction des intérêts personnels qu'ils trouvent dans leurs relations clandestines » voir *Le Jour* et *La Nouvelle Expression* parutions du 06 Mai 2022.

individuels relevant non pas du Code pénal, mais d'une conception de la morale qui n'est celle des magistrats concernés[43]. Or, « le tribunal n'est pas le gardien de l'ordre moral, mais celui du droit et de sa bonne application »[44]. En matière judiciaire, la morale a souvent le visage des évidences trop faciles et les oripeaux de la présomption de culpabilité[45]. Un auteur faisait remarquer que « rendre justice au quotidien, c'est un choix de vie. Il exige de construire sa légitimité dans la connaissance de la loi commune et dans la pugnacité au service de la vérité, puis dans la pratique sans cesse renouvelée de l'écoute contradictoire de chaque partie au procès, de leurs avocats et enfin dans l'humilité face aux choses de la vie qui vous sont soumises. Il faut accepter de douter, de regretter, de changer »[46].

2.1.2. Le souhait d'un modèle harmonieux des rapports entre magistrats et avocats

Le processus de recrutement des magistrats camerounais et des avocats n'est pas homogène[47] ce qui explique la défiance observée entre ces deux corps de métiers. Les juges et les avocats qui se côtoient au palais de justice n'ont pas la même histoire et les mêmes repères. Si certains ont fréquenté les

---

[43] Les deux premiers ont été condamnés le 11 mai 2021 à 5ans de prison ferme en vertu de la loi interdisant les relations homosexuelles parce qu'elles étaient vêtues de manière typiquement féminine. Quant à Martin Camus Mimb c'est une sextape qui le conduit à son inculpation sans qu'on puisse comprendre en quoi il a été complice de la publication provenant d'un téléphone ne lui appartenant pas. On peut imaginer sa personnalité en tant qu'analyste sportif dont le reproche ne pouvait consister que celui d'avoir participer à trois dans son bureau à des rapports sexuels. Ce qui sur le plan moral peut être reprochable mais pas sur le plan du droit.

[44] DUPOND- MORETTI, E., et DURAND- SOUFFLAND, S., *Directs du droit*, Michel Lafon, 2017, p.75.

[45] DUPOND- MORETTI, E., et DURAND- SOUFFLAND, S., Bête noire « condamner à plaider », Lafon 2012, p. 110.

[46] JOLY-COZ, G., « Qui est mon juge? », *In* : Robert SALIS (s.dir) *Rendre la justice* Calmann Levy, 2021 p.311.

[47] Voir supra.p.6 & 7.

mêmes universités il n'en est pas de même des écoles de formation. Ils semblent ne pas appartenir au même monde. Les avocats nourrissent donc en eux la frustration de ne pas participer au processus de décision judiciaire. Pour y parvenir, on pourrait s'inspirer du modèle du droit anglais.

En effet, il n'y a pas de véritable séparation entre les professions de juge et de *barrister*[48]. Cette homogénéité se traduit par un certain nombre de règles procédurales que la spécificité du monde judiciaire anglais a généré. Ainsi, les Juges anglais sont peu nombreux et comptent largement sur les avocats pour leur présenter les affaires de manière à économiser un temps précieux. Le juge anglais ne prépare pas l'audience et attend des avocats une présentation exhaustive de la jurisprudence pertinente. Il est d'ailleurs fréquent qu'il les remercie dans le jugement pour leur exposé[49]. La règle la plus frappante est celle selon laquelle le *barrister* est avant tout obligé envers le juge, et non envers son client. Ainsi, s'il apparait sans contradicteur devant une procédure d'ordonnance sur requête[50], le *barrister* est tenue d'une obligation d'objectivité. Il doit présenter les arguments que son adversaire aurait fait valoir s'il avait été présent. Si la procédure est rapide et nécessite une décision urgente, mais que les pièces sont très nombreuses, il doit aider le juge à identifier les plus pertinentes d'entre elles, qu'elles soient favorables ou défavorables à son client. Le *barrister* est tenu d'une « obligation de révélation complète et franche » [51] Il

---

48 La profession d'avocat en droit anglais est divisée professions : *les solicitors* et les *barristers.* Traditionnellement, la plaidoirie est réservée aux *barristers.* Les *sollicitors* fournissent en conséquence aux justiciables anglais toutes autres prestations juridiques notamment, le conseil et la rédaction d'acte.

49CUNIBERTI, G.,Grands systèmes de droit contemporains, LGDJ 4e edition, n°199, 2019, p. 111

50 L'ordonnance sur requête est une décision juridictionnelle provisoire rendue par un juge des requêtes dans les cas où les circonstances du litige justifient une dérogation au principe du contradictoire.

51 Full and frank disclosure, Form and substance in Anglo-American Law,

semble clair que de telles règles n'ont pu être consacrées par le droit judiciaire anglais qu'en raison de la confiance préexistante que les juges peuvent porter aux avocats plaidant devant eux. Cette approche de la défense n'est pas violente et offensive telle qu'on le vit aujourd'hui, elle permet d'éviter une crispation dans les relations entre avocats et magistrats, qui va souvent au-delà de celle qu'engendrait la défense de rupture de feu Jacques Vergès[52].

2.2. Dans le cadre des activités juridiques

En dehors des activités judicaires, la contribution de l'avocat à la justice est beaucoup plus visible dans les activités juridiques. En dehors de ses activités traditionnelles, il exerce réellement les missions de justice.

2.2.1. Des activités traditionnelles

On peut de prime abord évoquer le conseil et la consultation juridique qui sont des avis verbaux ou écrits donnés à un client à l'occasion d'un acte ou d'une action juridique ou judiciaire en vue d'éviter une difficulté ou un conflit à l'occasion d'un procès imminent ou en cours. Les consultations font partie des activités quotidiennes des avocats, lorsqu'elles sont délivrées par écrit, elles engagent directement leur responsabilité. Elles doivent donc être données et délivrées avec sérieux, compétence et conscience. La tâche de consultation est donc aussi importante que celle de procédure et de plaidoirie. En effet, l'avocat consultant est considéré comme le seigneur de la chicane. C'est à lui que songe Montesquieu dans *Lettres persanes* lorsqu'il fait dire par un homme en robe à son Persan « Nous avons des livres vivants, ce sont les avocats, ils travaillent pour nous et se chargent de notre culture ». Camus, dans ses lettres sur la

---

Oxford University Press, 1987, p.360 et s *In*: Gilles CUNIBERTI, op cit.

52 BOUAOUICHE, C., Magistrats-Avocats, duel ou duo? In Robert SALIS (s.dir). p.115.

profession, décrit le consultant comme une sorte de juge des affaires qu'on lui présente et sur la foi de l'avis duquel on se détermine à suivre une procédure ou à l'abandonner. Le législateur camerounais a pris en compte cette compétence avérée de l'avocat en matière de consultation, et pour démontrer sa contribution au processus décisionnel, il a exigé dans le Code de procédure civile et Commercial, qu'une consultation d'avocat soit demandée et produite notamment en cas de requête civile avant l'introduction de l'instance[53]. Dans ce cas la demande est assortie d'une consultation de trois avocats exerçant depuis cinq ans au moins devant les juridictions camerounaises.

L'avocat a aussi la possibilité d'établir tous les actes juridiques qui lui sont demandés de quelque nature que ce soit, sous réserve des restrictions légales ou règlementaires, notamment concernant les actes réservés à des professions déterminées. A cet effet, il rédige les actes, recueille le consentement des parties et procède aux formalités subséquentes. Dans la partie anglophone du pays l'avocat cumule les fonctions de notaire[54].

2.2.2. Des missions de justice

L'idée de la médiation ou la conciliation est le modèle dominant de résolution des litiges dans les droits traditionnels africains[55], mais aussi de toute civilisation depuis les premiers temps. Il suffit d'évoquer Plutarque opposé à tout juridisme excessif, saint Paul dans l'Epitre aux Corinthiens qui fait reproche aux chrétiens de ne pas faire arbitrer leurs différends

---

[53] Voir Art. 237 du Code de Procédure Civile et Commercial Camerounais.

[54] Voir article 74 de la loi organique « Les avocats installés dans les provinces su Sud-ouest et du Nord-ouest peuvent, à titre transitoire, exercer les fonctions de notaire.
Dans ce cas, leur compétence s'étend dans le ressort de la Cour d'Appel du siège de leur cabinet ».

[55] CUNIBERTI, G., *Grands systèmes de droit comparé,* LGDJ 4e édition, p. 396.

par l'un des leurs. Il en est de même en France sous l'Ancien Régime illustré par la phrase de Mazarin « Ce que tu peux régler pacifiquement ne cherche pas à le régler par la guerre ou un procès »[56].

De nouvelles possibilités de contribuer effectivement mais aussi efficacement à la qualité de la justice sont offertes aux avocats par les textes en matière de modes amiables de résolution des litiges. Elles offrent aux avocats la possibilité de résoudre les conflits sans passer par le juge notamment dans l'espace OHADA, eu égard à la volonté de développer la médiation dans le futur[57], nul doute que l'avocat trouvera une place de choix dans cette offre amiable. L'avocat peut également recevoir les missions d'arbitrage[58] avec la précision que l'avocat doit respecter « les règles particulières qui régissent la procédure arbitrale notamment les délais de procédure, de secret des délibérations ou encore observer lui-même et faire observer le principe de contradiction et de l'égalité de toutes les parties à l'instance ».

Dans d'autres systèmes de droit notamment en France, l'avocat peut être chargé de missions de praticien de droit collaboratif[59]. Celle-ci offre la possibilité aux avocats des parties d'orchestrer ensemble la procédure, auditionner les parties, les amener à s'écouter et comprendre avec elle la réalité de leur différend souvent éloignée de leurs premières déclarations et déduire l'objet de la preuve, recueillir si possible l'avis des experts qu'ils pourront désigner. Les avocats pourront procéder ensemble à l'audition des témoins, procéder à des constatations allant jusqu'à l'interprétation des

---

56 KEIME-ROBERT-HOUDIN, B., « Ombres et lumières de la médiation civile », In Robert SALIS (s.dir). p.323.

57 Voir Acte Uniforme OHADA relatif à la médiation adopté le 23 Novembre 2017 à Conakry.

58 Voir article 74.3 du Règlement Intérieur.

59 RIVET, T., (S.dir), *Déontologie de la profession d'Avocat*, LGDJ 4e édition 2021 n°565, p. 241

faits si celle-ci apparaissait incontestable aux parties, aidant ainsi à cibler le litige plutôt qu'à le disperser.

Désormais avec ces nouveaux procédés d'administration de la preuve ou de résolution des litiges pratiqués à la grande échelle, les accords, si rares auparavant, seraient ramassés à la pelle, comme des fruits tombés de l'arbre. L'heure ne serait plus aux « conclusions fleuves » destinées à perdre le juge pour masquer la faiblesse du dossier[60]. Les conclusions seraient construites dans un cadre méthodologique faisant apparaitre le raisonnement juridique. Les imprécisions seraient ainsi bannies. L'appel serait rarement interjeté même si la possibilité sera toujours offerte.

En matière pénale, les avocats vont acquérir en technicité et seront capables de soutenir des projets muris avec le prévenu, fondés sur des garanties sérieuses de réinsertion à l'appui de propositions de peines crédibles et adaptées. On pense ainsi aux peines alternatives introduites dans le droit camerounais par la loi n°2016-007 du 12 juillet 2016 portant Code pénal[61].

---

60 LE BRETON DE VANNOISE, R., « Un rêve d'humanité pour la justice », *In :* Robert SALIS (s.dir). p.357.

61 SOWENG, D., « L'introduction des peines alternatives en droit pénal camerounais, *in : juridis périodique* » n°113 janvier-février-mars 2018, pp 61 à 74.

Les mutations contemporaines de la guerre

Par

Abel Hubert Mback Wara

Département de Science Politique
Faculté des Sciences Juridiques et politiques
Université de Douala
ambackwara@gmail.com

Résumé

La guerre, cet acte de violence organisée entre unités politiques, se concevait originellement dans le cadre d'une confrontation militaire. Pourtant, l'utilisation contemporaine de technologies civiles à des fins militaires, concomitante avec un usage létal d'objets et de ressources à priori non militaires rendent compte d'une extension de la notion de guerre au-delà du champ militaire. Au-delà du champ de bataille, la guerre peut être observée partout où les antagonismes donnent lieu à l'expression d'une violence organisée entre unités politiques Cet article se propose donc, en recourant aux catégories des études critiques de la sécurité, de recenser les principales mutations contemporaines de la guerre.

Mots-clés : Guerre, Mutations, Informations, Economie

Introduction

Carl Von Clausewitz (1832 : I-1-2) définit la guerre comme étant *« un acte de violence ayant pour but de contraindre un adversaire à accomplir notre volonté »*. Deux éléments permettent de la caractériser qui sont, d'une part, l'usage de la violence létale et, d'autre part, la prégnance d'une volonté de domination politique. La guerre est une réalité inhérente aux sociétés humaines avec lesquelles elle évolue (Keegan 2014). En effet, si les guerres conventionnelles d'envergure telles que menées par les grandes puissances militaires semblent en passe de s'éteindre (Mack, 2007: 1) la guerre elle-même telle qu'en elle-même se porte mieux que jamais et est entrée dans une nouvelle phase (Creveld 1998). s'il est vrai que des évolutions ont été observées dans la conduite des opérations qui sont induites par la Révolution dans les Affaires Militaires (RAM) (Gray 2005), l'adoption de procédés asymétriques, l'émergence de nouveaux acteurs guerriers infra étatiques et transnationaux (Kaldor, 2012:3), et le recours aux sociétés militaires privées (Avant, 2008 :438-452) , il ne demeure pas moins vrai que la conception essentielle et fondamentale de la guerre a elle-même connu des transformations. Le phénomène martial se manifeste désormais sous des apparences autres que ses aspects militaires originels.

L'analyse de la polémologie contemporaine donne en effet d'observer une extension des affrontements dans des champs et selon des procédés inédits avec cependant les mêmes résultats, à savoir, l'effondrement des institutions, des organisations politiques, des acteurs de la scène nationale et internationale. La notion de guerre s'est étendue au-delà de l'affrontement militaire et peut être observée partout où les antagonismes donnent lieu à une violence organisée entre unités politiques (Bull, 1977:178). L'utilisation de technologies civiles à des fins militaires, concomitante avec un usage létal d'objets et de ressources à priori non militaires démontrent l'existence d'une diversité de formes alternatives de guerres. La question qui se pose alors est celle de savoir s'il est possible de procéder à une recension des mutations contemporaines de la guerre. En réponse à cette question, cet article se propose, en recourant aux catégories des études critiques de sécurité, de procéder à une requalification des principaux avatars contemporains de la guerre. La théorie criticiste a démontré sa capacité à fournir une conception pertinente de la sécurité parce que encrée sur la contextualité spatio-temporelle et débarrassée de toutes idées reçues, de tout à priori. En l'espèce, l'adoption d'une posture criticiste nous porte à poser que l'accroissement des frontières de la sécurité au-delà du champ de la défense militaire (Barry Buzan, 1991), induit un élargissement des limites notionnelles de la guerre au-delà de la confrontation militaire. Notre élaboration aura donc pour objectif de sérier les principaux modes alternatifs de la belligérance moderne selon qu'ils se déploient dans les dimensions intangibles des données et des idées(I) ou dans l'ordre tangible des moyens économiques (II).

1. Les guerres intangibles

L'importance de l'information en tant que moyen d'action est démontrée par le fait que la quasi-totalité des puissances militaires contemporaines ont intégré dans leur concept d'emploi des forces, un volet *information warfare ou* infoguerre, dispensé en enseignement dans les académies militaires mais aussi représenté dans les organigrammes des systèmes nationaux de défense. L'information constitue un véritable substitut fonctionnel des armes de guerres dans les champs de l'information et de la communication (A) d'une part, et dans l'espace numérique (B) d'autre part.

1.1. Propagande, Communication et guerre des idées

Le terme information vient du latin *Informare* qui signifie « donner une forme à » et renvoie au procédé d'agencement des différents éléments communicationnels rendant compte d'un phénomène. L'information est de ce point structurée non seulement par la perspective à partir de laquelle le phénomène est observé par l'informateur mais aussi par la perspective à partir de laquelle cette information est mise en forme et transmise. Cette double structuration de l'information est l'occasion d'un usage belliciste de celle-ci tant dans le champ militaire que civil.

1.1.1. La guerre par l'information : Les usages bellicistes de la communication

Le renseignement occupe une place prépondérante dans la conduite des engagements opérationnels. Clausewitz (1832: VI) définit le renseignement comme étant, *« toute la connaissance que nous pouvons avoir de l'ennemi et de son pays ; ils constituent donc la base sur laquelle s'appuient nos idées et nos actions »*. C'est dire qu'un renseignement est toute information qui permet et facilite la décision en réduisant le brouillard de l'incertitude qui inhibe les capacités d'action ou de réaction des unités engagées. Au sein des engagements militaires l'information est donc, à plus d'un titre, une arme. Elle est dans le cas de la transmission[1], *« l'arme qui unit les armes »*[2] et permet une cohérence de la manœuvre. Elle est dans l'éventualité du renseignement, ce multiplicateur de force majeur qui garantit une intervention rapide et précise, donc efficace. L'intelligence et le renseignement ne constituent donc pas que des moyens d'action, ils sont de véritables armes pouvant servir comme telles. L'importance de l'information est davantage marquée dans la nouvelle dimension de

[1] La transmission est l'arme de soutien spécialisée dans la mise en œuvre des systèmes d'information et de communication (SIC) militaires

[2] Telle est la devise de la transmission

l'engagement opérationnel qu'est l'action psychologique, la *guerre du sens*[3] ou encore la *guerre des perceptions*[4] . L'avènement de ce champ nouveau fait suite au renforcement de la dimension psychologique de la guerre encore considérée très marginalement jusque-là, et à une plus grande implication des médias dans la manœuvre. En effet, dans les guerres contemporaines, *« l'affrontement est autant psychologique que physique: la haine, le courage, le jusqu'au-boutisme mais aussi la terreur, la tromperie et le viol des esprits en constituent le moteur. L'art de faire adhérer, de désinformer ou de tromper prend le pas sur l'art de manœuvrer les forces»* (Francart, 2000). C'est à ce titre que l'"information et le renseignement sont classés parmi les éléments intangibles d'évaluation de la puissance des Etats.

Dans une autre perspective et en dehors du champ opérationnel, l'intelligence et le renseignement constituent de véritable ressource auxquelles l'entrepreneur politique recourt pour atteindre ses objectifs de domination (Lacam, 1998 : 27). Il est en effet des informations qui, du simple fait de leur détention ou leur divulgation causent l'effondrement des institutions étatiques, la disqualification d'acteurs politiques nationaux ou même internationaux. Dans ces circonstances aussi, l'information est le moyen par lequel certains acteurs de la scène internationale et même nationale parviennent à mettre leurs adversaires-ennemis hors-jeu, à les réduire à l'impuissance ou au silence. Du *Watergate*[5] aux *pandora papers*[6]

---

3 D'après un concept élaboré par Loup Francart (2000)

4 Cette notion fait référence la confrontation des avis et des opinions autour d'un conflit. Encore appelée action psychologique ou guerre du sens, la guerre de perceptions consiste dans toutes les actions visant à influencer positivement ou négativement la perception que nous avons de la légitimité de l'entreprise d'une des partie au conflit. Pour approfondir cette question, lire Loup FRANCART op. cit.

5 Le scandale du Watergate est une affaire d'espionnage politique qui aboutit, en 1974, à la démission de Richard Nixon, alors président des États-Unis.

6 *Pandora Papers* est une affaire de fuite d'environ 11,9 millions de documents faisant état de fraude et d'évasion fiscale à très large échelle.

en passant par le *Monicagate*[7] ou l'affaire *Clearstream*[8] la preuve est donnée du potentiel de létalité symbolique détenu par certaines informations et de l'usage belliqueux qui peut en découler.

1.1.2. La guerre de l'information, Les médias et la manipulation des consciences

La propagande est définie par Jacques Ellul (1990 :75) comme étant *« l'ensemble des méthodes utilisées par un groupe organisé en vue de faire participer activement ou passivement à son action une masse d'individus psychologiquement unifiées par des manipulations psychologiques et encadrés dans une organisation »*. Bien qu'elle se manifeste avec une intensité différente selon qu'on est en démocratie où elle est moins prégnante (Beauvois, 2005), ou dans les dictatures où elle est plus coercitive, la propagande reste une activité commune à tous les régimes politiques dans lesquels elle contribue à la fabrication du consentement (Herman et Chomsky, 2002). A ce titre, la propagande correspond aux critères distinctifs et définitionnels de la

---

Plusieurs milliers de personnalités y sont identifiés, dont trois cents responsables publics, trente-cinq chefs d'État et cent trente milliardaires directement mis en cause. Cf.
https://fr.wikipedia.org/wiki/Pandora_Papers consulté le 27/05/2022 à 11:12

7 Du nom de Monica Lewinsky, une femme d'affaires américaine qui a défrayé la chronique en 1998-1999 lorsqu'il a été rendu public qu'elle a eu des relations sexuelles avec le président Bill Clinton, lors d'un stage effectué à la Maison-Blanche. Le mensonge sous serment de Clinton à propos de cette relation conduit à un *impeachment* à son encontre, procédure qui est bloquée par le Sénat des États-Unis. Cf. https://fr.wikipedia.org/wiki/Monica_Lewinsky consulté le 27/05/2022 à 14:23

8 Le scandale financier *Clearstream*, du nom de la société financière luxembourgeoise, est déclenché par le journaliste Denis Robert et implique des personnalités politiques telles que Dominique De Villepin ou Nicolas Sarkozy dans un procès pour évasion fiscale et blanchiment d'argent. C'est aussi le théâtre de manipulations dans l'affaire des frégates de Taïwan. Cf. https://www.lefigaro.fr/actualite-france/dossier/affaire-clearstream, Consulté le 27/05/2022 à 12: 45

guerre que sont le recours à la violence comme moyen et la quête de domination politique comme fin. Ainsi, au-delà d'être un préambule à la guerre, la propagande est elle-même une instance de guerre dont la violence découle du discours, des images et des symboles qu'elle mobilise. Dans les cas extrêmes, la propagande est mise à contribution dans des processus de criminalisation du politique où elle concourt à la fabrication de l'ennemi, c'est-à-dire à l'utilisation de l'information dans la perspective de la construction, dans les perceptions, d'un ennemi à combattre. Observons, de façon non-exhaustive et à titre d'illustration, que les génocides Arménien[9], Juif et Tutsi[10] n'ont été rendus possibles que grâce à une propagande politique décrivant dans chaque cas les victimes comme de véritables fléaux à éradiquer.

Tout comme l'émission, la transmission de l'information est devenue l'occasion d'une bataille rangée au sein de laquelle les médias occupent les premières lignes. *« Les manipulations de l'information, qui ont toujours existé, sont aujourd'hui à la fois plus nombreuses et plus graves car elles sont véhiculées par des réseaux sociaux […] dans un climat de crise de confiance dans lequel la parole publique est dévaluée et la notion même de vérité est remise en cause »* (Jeangène, 2021 : i). L'affrontement entre les Chaines *Sputnik* et *Russia Today* d'une part, *Euronews* et *BBC* d'autre part, autour de la crise en Ukraine démontre à suffisance que, l'émission autant que la réception d'information peuvent faire l'objet de manipulations dont les conséquences peuvent se révéler fatales. Sur cette base, *« les régimes autoritaires, comme les démocraties libérales, ne perçoivent plus seulement l'information comme un instrument de rayonnement, mais aussi comme une source de vulnérabilité »* (Marangé et Quessard, 2021 :8). Dans l'ordre interne comme sur la scène internationale, la maitrise de

---

[9]Ce fut le cas notamment pour les génocides Arméniens cf. https://www.herodote.net/24_avril_1915-evenement-19150424.php,

[10] Pour plus de détails sur ces questions lire Régine Waintrater (2016) et Scholastique Mukasonga (2014)

l'information est devenue une ressource de puissance servant les projets de domination.

Mieux que vaincre, les médias permettent de convaincre. Le champ médiatique est ainsi devenu le lieu d'une manœuvre ou d'une stratégie selon l'échelle, où des acteurs s'affrontent à coups d'images et de scoops dans le but de créer dans les esprits des dispositions qui soient favorables à leurs prétentions et à leurs actions. *« Désormais, tout acte de destruction - et ses inévitables dommages collatéraux -est rapidement porté devant le tribunal de l'opinion publique internationale [...] or, les sociétés avancées sont fragiles devant les pertes et la violence projetées en boucle sur les écrans domestiques. »* (Desportes, 2006 :6). Les images choquent, émeuvent, bousculent et renversent au point de créer dans les consciences les conditions d'une adhésion, d'une désapprobation ou même d'une condamnation.

1.2. L'espace numérique et la cyberguerre

De l'avis de Martin Motte (2018 :305), *« l'extension de la conflictualité [...] gagne parallèlement un nouveau domaine au fur et à mesure que croît l'utilisation de données numériques et que s'établit entre leurs utilisateurs une véritable dialectique, faite alternativement de coopération et d'affrontement : l'espace numérique ou cyberespace »*. En d'autres termes, le cyberespace se transforme au fur et à mesure de son utilisation et de son évolution, en un véritable champ de bataille où se recensent des actions d'une violence inouïe.

1.2.1. La jungle cyber spatiale

Le cyberespace est, à bien des points, semblable à *l'état de nature* de Thomas Hobbes, cet état de guerre permanente où, l'homme étant un loup pour l'homme, il prévaut de façon permanente une guerre de tous contre tous. Il faut relever au préalable que le numérique est la concrétisation d'intentions libérales. Il s'agissait au départ de mettre en contact les chercheurs de divers horizons, puis de connecter les opérateurs économiques en se fondant sur le principe que *« la connectivité est préférée à la sécurité »* (Salamon 2020 :21). Selon une topologie admise, l'espace numérique est composé de trois couches successives comprenant une couche physique[11] faite d'appareils numériques tangibles localisables et cartographiable, une couche logique constituée de *« protocoles de routage et d'adressage qui permettent aux paquets de données d'atteindre leur destination sans se perdre et en minimisant les risques de congestion »* (Limonier 2021 : 61), et enfin, une couche sémantique ou cognitive *« qui est plus spécifiquement en rapport avec le contenu informationnel. En clair, l'ensemble des messages qui passe par Internet »* (Taillat, 2018 :30). Le cyberespace s'est créé en s'affirmant très tôt comme un espace libertaire c'est-à-dire un espace privilégiant l'anonymat et l'absence de toute forme de surveillance. En effet, *« pensé dès l'origine comme un système décentralisé, Internet est un maillage dépourvu d'autorité centrale unique »* (Salamon, Op cit : 22). Dans les faits, le cyberespace est composé d'un ensemble de systèmes d'origines et de nationalités diverses, reliés les uns aux autres par une série de connexions physiques et de protocoles de routage. Dans cette configuration, tous les systèmes restent liés, mais aucun système ne prédomine sur les autres. Le cyberespace est un univers exempt d'une autorité uniforme et prégnante. Certes quelques instances[12] auto-proclamées en assurent la

---

[11] Cette couche encore appelée couche basse est composée *« des terminaux (smartphones, ordinateurs…) qui permettent d'avoir accès à l'information, [...] des infrastructures où les informations que l'on souhaite consulter sont physiquement inscrites (serveurs) […,] les câbles transocéaniques, les dorsales de fibre optique, ainsi que les satellites permettant de faire transiter cette information entre le receveur et l'hébergeur de la donnée »*. (Limonier 2021 : 61)

[12] Sous cette rubrique l'on peut ranger : *Internet Society* (ISOC), association de droit américain qui promeut le développement, l'évolution et l'usage d'Internet ; *Internet Architecture Board* (IAB), groupe informel chapeauté par l'ISOC en charge du développement technique ; *Internet Engineering Task Force* (IETF), groupe informel dépendant de l'IAB travaillant à l'élaboration et à la promotion de standards techniques tels que TCP/IP ; *Internet Corporation for Assigned Names and Numbers* (ICANN), société de droit californien à but non lucratif, chargée de l'administration de l'adressage IP et de la gestion des treize serveurs DNS dits « racines » ; Les

coordination mais cela reste en dehors de tout consensus démocratique qui puisse légitimer cette autorité. Par sa configuration, l'espace numérique pose donc un problème de souveraineté traduit en termes de contrôle et de protection de l'intégrité des infrastructures numériques et des informations transitant dans les réseaux. En effet, à côté du désir de certains Etats[13] de contrôler la masse d'informations qui entre et sort de leurs sphères de souveraineté territoriale, il y a les inquiétudes des usagers de voir les informations liées à leurs propriétés et à leurs vies privées sauvegardées et protégées.

1.2.2. La bellicité du cyber espace

« À l'ère numérique, la protection des flux d'information et des infrastructures dédiées est devenue un enjeu de sécurité majeur pour tous les dirigeants » (Marangé et Quessard, Op cit : 17). C'est dire que le cyberespace est devenu un champ de bataille où une diversité d'actions offensives est enregistrée qui vise à porter un coup fatal aux systèmes pris pour cible.

Par définition, une cyber-attaque consiste en une utilisation malveillante de l'espace numérique. Une cyber-attaque prend forme « *lorsque qu'une entité attaquante effectue un enchaînement d'actions via des voies numériques ou physiques pour exploiter les propriétés du cyberespace (notamment ses vulnérabilités, techniques ou structurelles), afin de réaliser des impacts, eux-mêmes d'ordre numérique ou physique* » (Salamon, op cit : 56-57). En règle générale, les attaques dans l'espace numérique sont principalement de deux types. Les attaques peuvent être physiques et porter sur les infrastructures et équipements constituant le réseau

---

cinq *Regional Internet Registry* (RIR), qui allouent les blocs d'adresses IP dans chacune des cinq zones du monde dans lesquelles ils sont situés ; *Internet Governance Forum* (IGF), sous tutelle de l'ONU, qui est le grand forum mondial sur la gouvernance d'Internet.

13 Dans cette rubrique on peut citer la Russie pour qui la « souveraineté informationnelle » doit être protégée au même titre que l'intégrité territoriale ; La Chine, la Corée du Nord, l'Iran, les Etats Unis, Israël et le Japon.

numérique. Il peut s'agir pour le cas d'espèce d'une rupture des câbles[14] avec pour conséquence la déconnection de toute une zone territoriale du réseau, ou d'une manipulation malveillante des routeurs BGP[15] aboutissant à un détournement des *datas* vers une destination territoriale non voulue au départ. Les cyber-attaques sont diverses[16] et plus fréquentes dans la couche logicielle ou logique. Dans cette dimension, les attaques peuvent prendre la forme de codes élaborés pour s'introduire frauduleusement dans un système, en provoquer la modification, le dysfonctionnement, la paralysie, ou en extraire des données. De même, les acteurs ou commanditaires de ces attaques relèvent des statuts les plus divers et vont des Etats[17], aux individus en passant par les sociétés et organisations privées et même le crime organisé. À cause de la diversité des possibilités d'attaques, *« la conflictualité dans le cyberespace présente une asymétrie forte entre l'attaque et la défense. La partie attaquante n'a théoriquement besoin d'exploiter qu'une seule faille, d'un seul système, sur une temporalité relativement courte, pour réussir à mener à bien son action »* (Salamon, Op Cit : 29-30). La bellicité de l'espace numérique ne découle pas uniquement des actions offensives qui y sont menées. Elle se fonde plus sur le potentiel de dévastation que ces actions ont

---

14 Ce fut le cas en en 2008, lorsque les câbles reliant Sotchi au port géorgien de Poti furent débranchés et en 2014 lorsque, les câbles reliant la Crimée à l'Ukraine continentale *via* l'isthme de Perekop furent mis hors d'état de fonctionner par les forces russes.

15 le Border Gateway Protocol (BGP) est un protocole d'échange de route externe utilisé notamment sur le réseau Internet. Son objectif principal est d'échanger des informations de routage et d'accessibilité de réseaux entre systèmes autonomes. Cf. https://fr.wikipedia.org/wiki/Border_Gateway_Protocol consulté le 16/09/2022 à 20:18

16 Il peut s'agir, de façon non exhaustive de virus, du *Hacking*, du *phishing* d'un cheval de Troie

17 On peut citer ici la cyber-attaque menée en 2007 contre l'administration estonienne par des agents russes, ou l'attaque lancée par les Etats Unis contre le programme nucléaire iranien au moyen du maliciel *Stuxnet.* Pour plus de détails consulter Yann Salamon op cit, pp 83-90

sur leurs cibles. Les attaques menées dans l'espace numérique peuvent être constitutives d'actes de guerre en ceci qu'elles portent atteinte à l'intégrité fonctionnelle de certains systèmes considérés comme vitaux même pour des Etats. L'intégrité des systèmes numériques peut être engagée non seulement en violant la confidentialité[18] des informations contenues mais aussi en altérant de façon partielle ou totale le fonctionnement[19] même de ces systèmes de données. Au-delà du coût élevé que ces actes peuvent causer en termes de dommages matériels, il faut envisager la perte de crédibilité qu'elles suscitent surtout pour les acteurs tels les banques dont le statut repose sur la confiance. Ainsi, le cyberespace est un milieu qui, par son architecture ouverte, est propice à des approches indirectes qui privilégient *« l'attaque des sources de la puissance adverse [et qui] consiste à surprendre, déséquilibrer et désorganiser l'adversaire, [elle] recherche la victoire par l'effondrement plus que par la destruction en utilisant les voies les moins prévisibles »* (France/Armée de Terre, 2008 : 48-49).

2. L'économie et la guerre des ressources tangibles

Les ressources matérielles ne sont plus uniquement des motifs de guerre, elles sont devenues des véritables moyens par lesquels les acteurs recherchent l'effondrement du dispositif adverse. Après les guerres pour l'or ou le pétrole, on

---

18 À compter de mars 2017, une divulgation massive de documents classifiés concernant la CIA a été relayée par la plate-forme *Wikileaks*, sous le nom de code « *Vault 7* ». Plus de 8 000 documents ont été publiés de façon hebdomadaire à compter du 23 mars 2017. Au-delà des conséquences néfastes sur les relations diplomatiques des Etats Unis avec plusieurs pays, il faut relever au plan interne l'impact négatif en termes de violation du secret-défense.

19 Fin avril 2007, une série de cyberattaques par déni de service a paralysé l'Estonie. De nombreux services en ligne, comme ceux des plus grandes institutions bancaires du pays, *Hansapank* et *SEB Eesti Uhispank*, ont ainsi été contraints à la fermeture de même que plusieurs services publics ont été paralysés pendant des jours.

assiste plus fréquemment à la guerre par l'or, le pétrole. Les ressources matérielles, fruits de l'activité économique, sont devenues de véritables armes létales.

La guerre économique

Le concept de guerre économique renvoie à toute action ou procédé économique dont le but à terme est l'effondrement ou la disparition du dispositif de production de distribution ou de consommation de biens et services d'un adversaire préalablement désigné comme tel. *« Dans la guerre économique, le sang ne coule pas, la lutte n'est pas forcément sanglante mais elle est violente et il y a bien des armes. Non pas des fusils des revolvers, des canons ou des tanks, mais des armes plus subtiles comme des OPA, des intrusions informatiques, de l'espionnage, du chantage, de la corruption...»* (Laïdi, 2012 : 19). En d'autres termes, les interactions entre acteurs économiques, sans être sanglantes, peuvent être d'une violence qui est telle qu'elle se résume sinon à des pertes en vies humaines, du moins à l'élimination de composantes des dispositifs économiques en confrontation.

2.1. Les Acteurs

Pour Ali Laïdi (Op Cit : 13) la guerre économique est *« la stratégie et le comportement économiques agressifs d'une entreprise, d'un État, d'une ONG ou de tout groupement humain pour atteindre un objectif : conquérir ou protéger des parts de marché. Il y a guerre économique lorsqu'un de ces acteurs use de moyens déloyaux ou illégaux pour atteindre son objectif »*. En fournissant une telle définition de la guerre économique, Laïdi nous donne un aperçu de la diversité des acteurs engagés dans ce type de guerre et qui peuvent être regroupés en acteurs institutionnels publics et en acteurs privés.

2.1.1. Les entreprises et firmes privées

La question de la nationalité des entreprises multinationales qui reste au cœur de la définition du statut guerrier de ces entreprises constitue une véritable pomme de discorde entre les courants libéraux et leurs adversaires. Tandis que les libéraux considèrent que la nationalité est improductive et peu prégnante parce que diluée par la mondialisation, les communautaristes arguent que les firmes multinationales restent sous la tutelle du seul détenteur de la souveraineté démocratique qu'est l'Etat et dont elles reçoivent en outre la protection. Au-delà de ce débat d'idéologies, la pratique nous donne de constater qu'à plusieurs occurrences, même dans les démocraties libérales les plus avancées, les firmes sont considérées comme des composantes de la puissance et du rayonnement de l'Etat et reçoivent à ce titre tout l'accompagnement et l'assistance dont elles ont besoin. En un mot, les entreprises multinationales restent liées à leur nationalité. Bien plus, ce lien de nationalité est le fondement d'interactions très violentes entre Etats au travers de leurs multinationales. Dans les faits, les entreprises remplacent les divisions ; le capital, la puissance de feu, les garnisons à l'étranger sont les filiales des multinationales et les marchés financiers se transforment en armes nucléaires. La quête et la conservation de la souveraineté économique place ainsi les multinationales en première ligne d'un affrontement dont les pratiques sont les Offres Publiques d'Acquisition (OPA)[20], l'espionnage économique, les lois protectionnistes[21] ou les subventions de tous genres rendant la concurrence déloyale et malsaine. Dans tous ces cas, les conséquences se résument en une élimination des entreprises victimes soit du fait du

[20] Une OPA est une opération par laquelle un acquéreur potentiel indique publiquement aux actionnaires d'une société qu'il est prêt à acheter leur titre à un prix supérieur aux cours cotés en bourse en vue de s'assurer le contrôle de la majorité de la société sans avoir recours à des achats successifs en bourse ou à une cession directe d'action.

[21] En 2006, le projet « ciel ouvert » entre les États-Unis et l'Union européenne a été bloqué par une décision de la Maison-Blanche qui a refusé que la part des investisseurs étrangers dans les compagnies aériennes puisse dépasser les 25 %

discrédit, du démantèlement après rachat[22], de leur absorption[23] ou de la faillite.

2.1.2. L'Etat

La guerre économique est certes menée au premier plan par les entreprises et firmes multinationales mais elle est en fait commanditée par les Etats. Dans cette perspective, la guerre économique est « *l'affrontement que se livrent les Etats-nations pour s'assurer le contrôle des « ressources rares » nécessaires à leur économie* » (Gauchon, 2011 :659). L'économie étant un enjeu majeur de puissance structurelle[24], la protection du statut et des intérêts des Etats passe inévitablement par des actions de protection et de projection des entreprises nationales sur le marché international. En fait, la prégnance des intérêts économiques nationaux oblige les États à participer aux batailles économiques, officiellement pour réglementer les marchés et officieusement pour soutenir leurs champions nationaux. Dans le détail, l'Etat peut intervenir de

---

22 En 2009 l'entreprise Plysorol, n°2 du contreplaqué européen est rachetée par les firmes chinoises Longsheng et Honest Timber Gabon, intéressées par les concessions d'Okoumé de Plysorol au Gabon. Les acquéreurs organisent ensuite sa cessation de paiement et démantèle la société pour n'en conserver que les droits sur les 600 000 hectares d'okoumé. Cf. https://www.lesechos.fr/2014/09/lespoir-decu-des-salaries-de-plysorol-291935

23 A titre d'illustration, le groupe Blue Star filiale du groupe d'Etat China National Chemical Corporation, qui a racheté l'activité silicones de Rhodia Silicones, alors leader mondial dans le secteur. Blue Star a ensuite construit en Chine une unité de production d'une capacité égale à celle de tous les sites européens réunis. Le même groupe Blue Star a appliqué la même méthode au Français Adisseo, troisième producteur mondial de méthionine, utilisé dans la nutrition animale, et a construit à Nanjing une usine de capacité supérieure à l'usine basée en France. Cf. Marie-Pierre Van Hoecke (2013)

24 Susan Strange définit la puissance structurelle comme étant « *la capacité de façonner et de déterminer les structures de l'économie politique globale au sein desquelles les autres Etats, leurs institutions politiques, leurs entreprises économiques et leurs scientifiques et autres experts doivent opérer* » Cf. Susan Strange citée par Marchesin,(2008 : 49)

façon directe dans le champ économique en apportant son soutien aux entreprises locales en les nationalisant[25] ou en les subventionnant lorsqu'elles sont en difficulté. L'Etat peut aussi générer un cadre normatif qui soit favorable aux entreprises nationales et défavorables aux entreprises étrangères[26]. L'Etat peut également soutenir les entreprises nationales en mettant les services de renseignement à contribution notamment dans le cadre de l'espionnage et du contre-espionnage économique. Allusion est ici faite aux *« systèmes d'intelligence nationaux qui permettent aux États de soutenir plus ou moins discrètement (notamment à l'export) leurs entreprises tout en surveillant la concurrence. Derrière la main invisible du marché, se cache l'État. Et, depuis quelques années, cette main est très active »*[27].

2.2. Les enjeux

L'activité économique est construite autour, d'une part des biens et services qui sont l'objet des transactions économiques et, d'autre part de la monnaie qui sert d'étalon de valeur de ces biens et services. La monnaie et les ressources constituent donc les principaux moyens de l'activité économique en général et de la guerre économique en particulier. L'économie n'est plus uniquement un motif de guerre, elle en est devenue une occurrence.

2.2.1. La monnaie

La monnaie est définie comme un instrument de mesure et de conservation de la valeur, et un moyen légal d'échange des

---

[25] En 2008, pour permettre à certaines entreprises de surmonter la crise des *subprimes*, la Maison-Blanche a du nationaliser des compagnies comme Fannie Mae, Freddie Mac, l'assureur AIG et General Motors, en injectant des milliards de dollars dans ces sociétés. Dans les mêmes circonstances, le gouvernement britannique a procédé à la nationalisation de la banque Northern Rock.

[26] Aux États-Unis, l'*amendement Exxon-Florio* autorise le président de la république à empêcher le rachat d'une firme américaine par des investisseurs étrangers si cette vente menace la sécurité nationale.

[27] Laïdi, A.,Les Etats en guerre économique, Paris, Seuil, 2010, P 121

biens. La monnaie est liée à un Etat et est en vigueur dans une zone monétaire déterminée. Par sa valeur sur les marchés de change, la monnaie est un indicateur du statut de puissance des Etats. Elle est de ce point une ressource de puissance mobilisée par les Etats dans leurs interactions parfois conflictuelles. La guerre des monnaies ou guerre des changes est ainsi une situation ou les Etats font s'affronter leurs monnaies avec pour objectif soit de crédibiliser leur monnaie nationale en faisant baisser son taux de change, soit de décrédibiliser les monnaies adverses à travers des attaques spéculatives. La guerre des monnaies peut prendre deux principaux aspects. Primo, elle peut être une guerre entre monnaies admises comme mode de règlement des transactions à l'échelle mondiale. Cette position de monnaie de référence qui a souvent été celle du Dollar américain est porteuse de nombreux avantages qui placent une telle monnaie en position d'hégémonie. Le statut de monnaie de réserve oblige les autres états à détenir des réserves de Dollars pour leurs transactions, toutes choses qui créent une demande permanente du Dollar sur le marché des devises. Ensuite, à travers les lois d'extraterritorialité, les Etats Unis ont trouvé le moyen de soumettre les opérateurs économiques qui utilisent le dollar à la législation américaine. A peine de sanctions ou d'amendes[28], les opérateurs qui utilisent le dollar doivent se soumettre aux dispositions du droit américain des affaires, ce qui crée un énorme préjudice pour les entreprises et les gouvernements concernés. A rebours et pour s'affranchir de cette prédominance du Dollar certains opérateurs choisissent de régler leurs transactions dans des devises autres que le dollar[29] contribuant ainsi à relativiser et à dévaloriser la monnaie américaine.

---

[28] En 2014 la banque BNP Paribas a été frappée d'une amende de 8,974 milliards de dollars pour violation d'embargos et de régimes de sanctions en ayant autorisés des flux financiers en dollars US par des entités sous sanctions.

[29] On peut ranger dans ce registre la décision prise par des pays comme

Secundo, la guerre des monnaies peut prendre l'aspect de manipulation du cours de la monnaie afin de renforcer la compétitivité de l'économie. En règle générale, une monnaie forte offre un pouvoir d'achat élevé vis à vis des produits étrangers et réduit le pouvoir d'achat étranger vis-à-vis de la production locale. Il s'en suit alors un déficit de la balance de commerce suscité par une augmentation des importations et une diminution concomitante des exportations. La pratique consiste dans ce cas de figure à dévaluer ou sous-évaluer la monnaie afin d'en susciter la dépréciation et de renforcer la compétitivité de l'économie locale. Ali Laïdi nous rappelle ainsi qu' *« États-Unis et Chine sont accusés de manipuler le cours de leur monnaie afin de protéger leur économie. Plus le dollar et le yuan sont bas, plus les entreprises américaines et chinoises sont compétitives à l'export »* (Laïdi, 2012: 12-13). En réalité, la dépréciation d'une monnaie provoque l'appréciation relative des autres monnaies et un déficit dans leurs balances de commerce. Pour éviter l'appréciation de leur monnaie et contrôler son taux de change, certains pays accumulent des réserves de change[30]. Une devise peut aussi faire l'objet d'attaques spéculatives soit par des banques centrales soit par des fonds vautour[31], le but

---

le Venezuela, la Russie, L'Inde ou l'Arabie Saoudite de régler leurs transactions en Yuan afin de s'affranchir de l'arbitraire du dollar

30 Les *réserves de change* désignent tous les **avoirs en devises et en or** détenus par les banques centrales, pour garantir le **cours de la monnaie nationale**, et pour financer les importations. Pour maîtriser le taux de change, les banques centrales peuvent acheter leur propre monnaie ou les devises qu'elles détiennent sur les marchés financiers, ou au contraire y vendre leur monnaie ou des devises. Cf. https://www.boursedescredits.com/lexique-definition-reserves-change-4078.php en ligne consulté le 11/08/2022 à 10:52

31 Les "fonds vautours" également appelés "fonds procéduriers" sont des fonds d'investissement apparus dans les années 1990, après la crise de la dette du tiers monde du début des années 1980, et au moment des allègements de dettes souveraines des pays pauvres très endettés. On les qualifie de "vautours", parce qu'ils acquièrent au rabais des dettes de pays dont l'économie est en difficulté et qui sont proches du défaut de paiement, ou ont déjà fait défaut, dans le but d'engranger des profits

étant de faire perdre des réserves ou de susciter une plus-value sur les ordres de vente massive des devises. Dans tous les cas l'objectif final est une perte de compétitivité de l'économie adverse suite à une déstabilisation de son système monétaire.

2.2.2. Les ressources

En plus d'être un enjeu de guerre, les ressources économiques sont souvent mobilisées comme de véritables armes dans la bellicité internationale. Selon une définition de Bernadette Mérenne-Schoumaker[32], *« les matières premières correspondent aux produits miniers [...] aux produits énergétiques (y compris les agrocarburants), aux produits agricoles et de l'élevage, au bois et aux poissons »*. Il s'agit en d'autres termes de l'ensemble des ressources issues de l'élevage, du sol ou du sous-sol et susceptibles d'être consommés directement, utilisés dans la transformation de matériels finis ou comme source d'énergie. La guerre des matières premières est menée selon deux principaux procédés qui se résument à agir sur l'offre ou la demande des matières premières sur les marchés. Les mesures de coercition économiques prises contre un Etat pour bloquer son accès au marché peuvent consister soit en un embargo soit en un blocus. Tandis que l'embargo consister à empêcher ou restreindre certaines transactions, le blocus se résume à une interruption de toutes relations économiques ou financières avec un Etat. Qu'il s'agisse de l'embargo ou du blocus, le but de la manœuvre est de déstructurer l'économie adverse et de créer par effet de conséquence des désordres sociaux afin d'accentuer profondément la pression sur le pouvoir politique adverse. Woodrow Wilson estimait en son

---

exorbitants sur ces créances. Cf. Les « fonds vautours », *Dette et Développement* une publication de la Plateforme sur la dette des pays du Sud, en ligne disponible sur https://dette-developpement.org/IMG/pdf/4_pages_fonds_vautours.pdf consulté le 12//08/2022 à 08:42

32 Mérenne-Schoumaker, B., Atlas mondial des matières premières, Paris, Éditions Autrement, 2013, 2.

temps que, *« plus qu'un moyen de pression, l'embargo constituait, pour lui, à la fois une arme de guerre et un substitut de guerre »*[33]. Effectivement, bien que les sanctions économiques soient imposées en l'absence de coups de feu, elles produisent notamment au sein de la population autant de dégâts[34] que des armes de destruction massives. Les exemples de la Libye, de l'Iraq et du Soudan (Niblock, et Loulouwa, 2000 : 95-108) sont assez illustratifs par le nombre de victimes que ces sanctions ont générées et l'intensité énorme de la pression qu'elles ont fait peser sur les régimes politiques en place dans ces Etats. L'utilité géostratégique des sanctions est qu'en réduisant la marge de manœuvre des régimes au pouvoir, elles mettent les Etats ciblés dans une situation identique à celle dans laquelle ils seraient s'ils avaient perdu l'usage d'une frange considérable de leurs forces de défense et de sécurité. Dans ces cas, mieux que la coercition militaire, les sanctions économiques permettent d'emporter la décision et d'atteindre l'Etat Final Recherché (EFR).

En face des sanctions économiques, le contrôle et les restrictions offensives de la production constituent une autre alternative de la guerre économique. Dans les faits, un ou plusieurs Etats producteurs majeurs d'une ressource décident d'encadrer l'offre de ce produit en limitant la quantité de la production ou en excluant certains Etats de cette offre. L'objectif recherché étant de déstabiliser l'économie ciblée en y créant des pénuries, des hausses de prix, ce qui va engendrer des mouvements sociaux et, à terme, augmenter la pression sur le régime en place. C'est dans ce sens qu'il faut lire, en juillet 2022, l'arrêt de livraison par la Russie de gaz aux pays de l'Union Européenne, et l'ensemble des mesures d'austérité

---

33 Cité par Bernard Ferrand, (2004 : 58)

34 A titre d'illustration, en fin 2002, le ministère irakien de Santé publique, estimait que l'embargo contre l'Irak avait fait 1 806 915 victimes civiles, dont 750 000 enfants de moins de 5 ans. Cf. https://www.solidaire.org/articles/irak-25-ans-de-guerre-d-occupation-de-mort-et-de-destruction en ligne consulté le 19/08/2022 à 21 :08

énergétiques adoptées dans les pays d'Europe pour faire face à la crise énergétique[35] qui s'en est suivie.

Force reste cependant de rappeler que les mesures de guerre économique, pour être efficaces, doivent être suivies par la totalité des protagonistes de la scène internationale à défaut de quoi, elles produisent l'inverse de l'effet recherché par les initiateurs de la mesure. En effet, l'embargo ou le refus de livrer des ressources restent inefficace si l'Etat qui en est la cible a la possibilité, soit de livrer ses ressources à des acheteurs alternatifs dans le cas de l'embargo, soit d'acquérir cette ressource auprès d'autres Etats lorsqu'il s'agit d'une restriction d'offre. Bien plus, en considérant l'équilibre des prix déterminé par la règle de l'offre et de la demande, l'annonce des sanctions induisant une diminution de l'offre peut, suite à des spéculations, aboutir à une augmentation du prix de la ressource sur le marché mondial. En termes plus clairs, les violations de l'embargo ou du blocus procurent un avantage supplémentaire à l'Etat ciblé en ce sens qu'elles lui permettent, du fait de l'augmentation des prix, de gagner plus en vendant moins. C'est dans cet ordre d'idées qu'il faut situer les conclusions du rapport du Fonds Monétaire International (FMI)[36] de juillet 2022 selon lesquelles, suite à la crise en

---

[35] Parvenu au mois de juillet 2022, la Russie avait réduit de 60 % les livraisons de gaz aux pays Européens par Nord Stream. Malgré des efforts considérables pour réduire sa dépendance au gaz russe l'Allemagne est restée dépendante à 35 % de ses importations en la matière provenant de Russie, contre 55 % avant la guerre. Cf. https://www.ledevoir.com/monde/732366/gaz-russe-l-europe-plonge-dans-l-inconnu-avec-l-arret-temporaire-de-nord-stream consulté le 24/08/2022 à 21: 23

[36] *« Le volume de gaz russe acheminé par gazoduc vers l'Europe a fortement diminué, pour atteindre 40 % environ de son niveau d'il y a un an, ce qui a contribué à une forte hausse des cours du gaz naturel en juin. On estime que la contraction de l'économie russe au deuxième trimestre a été moindre que prévu, […] Dans le même ordre d'idées, les effets de la guerre sur les principaux pays européens ont été plus négatifs qu'anticipé du fait de la hausse des prix de l'énergie»*, Cf. Fond Monétaire International, *Perspectives de l'économie mondiale : un horizon sombre et plus incertain*, Juillet 2022,

Ukraine, les sanctions européennes contre la Russie ont causé plus de dommage aux économies européennes qu'à celle Russe.

Conclusion

A la question principale d'identifier et de recenser les avatars contemporains de la guerre, nous avons répondus en démontrant que les processus de guerre ont évolué et se sont complexifiés dans leurs formes tout en gardant le même fond, qui est celui de la déconstruction de l'adversité par tous les moyens possibles. La guerre prospère de nos jours en dehors du champ militaire. Elle se déploie notamment avec une prégnance certaine dans les champs intangibles des données et des idées autant que dans l'ordre tangible des moyens et des ressources de l'activité économique. La polémologie contemporaine donne de plus en plus l'occasion d'observer un usage guerrier de moyens originellement non militaires tels les informations, les datas, la monnaie et les matières premières, autant d'éléments qui constituent de véritables substituts fonctionnels aux armes de guerre. Assurément, la guerre a changé de visages parce que, face aux nouvelles menaces, les hommes se sont trouvés de nouvelles armes.

p 04, En ligne, disponible sur https://www.imf.org/-/media/Files/Publications/WEO/2022/Update/July/French/textf.ashx consulté le 01/09/2022 à 12:00

To Cooperate or not to Cooperate: African States' Uneasy Relationship with the International Criminal Court

By

Etienne Kentsa

Senior Lecturer, University of Buea

Abstract

The difficulties that emerged in the relationship between the ICC and Africa following the issuance of the arrest warrants for Omar al-Bashir and Muammar Gaddafi increase the relevance of questioning the legal basis for both the obligation and refusal to cooperate of African States with the ICC. First, the article elaborates on the obligation to cooperate based on the relevant provisions of the Rome Statute and postulates that it is an obligation principally borne by States Parties though specific provisions of the Statute state the obligation to cooperate of third States. Second, the article shows that this obligation can be created through ad hoc cooperation arrangements or agreements concluded by the Court and Non-Party States. The author also assesses the incorporation of the obligation to cooperate in eight African States Parties' laws, exposing their diversity with regard to the imperative nature of this obligation. He points out that the ICC lacks coercive power against requested States that fail to provide it assistance. Finally, the article discusses the legal grounds for refusal of African States to cooperate with the Court in relation to the Al-Bashir case. It postulates that the rules of international law relating to immunities of State officials and conflicting African regional law are reasons that could justify the denial of assistance in the arrest and surrender of Al-Bashir.

Key Words: Cooperate, Rome Statute, coercive power, obligation

Introduction

The International Criminal Court (hereafter "ICC") cannot function effectively without full cooperation of States. The importance of including a general obligation to cooperate in Article 86 of the Rome Statute is therefore understandable. This article is the result of a long process that dates back to 1994, with the International Law Commission (ILC)'s draft Statute,[1] Article 51(1) of which provided that: "*States Parties shall cooperate with the Court in connection with criminal investigations and proceedings under this Statute.*" This laid the groundwork for the future general obligation to cooperate. If the idea that States parties would be subject to an obligation to cooperate with the future Court was accepted, the same was not true of its substantial content. For instance, the Government of China considered that paragraph 1 of article 51 of the draft Statute was "*overly coercive, and* [did] *not grant the States parties the leeway they require for determining how much assistance they wish to provide in international criminal matters.*" It therefore suggested that this section should be rephrased to read "*shall make the utmost effort to cooperate.*"[2]

The general obligation to cooperate will be reaffirmed in all subsequent drafts.[3] However, Article 86 of the Rome

---

[1] Report of the International Law Commission on the Work of its Forty-Sixth Session, GAOR 49th Session Supp. No. 10, UN Doc. A/49/10 (1994).

[2] UNGA, *Ad Hoc* Committee on the establishment of an International Criminal Court, 3-13 April 1995, Comments received pursuant to paragraph 4 of GA Res. 49/53 on the establishment of an International Criminal Court, A/AC.244/1, 20 March 1995, p. 11, § 14.

[3] MBAYE, A. Z., and SHOAMANESH, S.S., « Article 86. Obligation générale de coopérer », in Julian FERNANDEZ and Xavier PACREAU (eds), *Statut de Rome de la Cour pénale internationale, Commentaire article par article*, Paris, Pedone, 2012, pp. 1791-1804 (p. 1791). For the drafting history of the general obligation to cooperate, See M. Cherif BASSIOUNI

Statute has gone the latter since it contains a "strict cooperation obligation"[4] since States concerned do not (in principle) have the latitude to cooperate or not to cooperate. Indeed, the obligation to cooperate with the ICC « *transcende le simple devoir moral des États envers la conscience universelle, pour s'ériger en cette obligation juridique contraignante dépassant, dans certains cas, le simple lien conventionnel tiré du Statut de Rome* »[5]. Even though the obligation to cooperate is not absolute,[6] it is worth noting that as per Article 26 of the Vienna Convention on the Law of Treaties (1969), "[e]*very treaty in force is binding upon the parties to it and must be performed by them in good faith.*" *Bona fide* performance of the Rome Statute with respect to cooperation and judicial assistance means that States concerned shall cooperate fully with the Court. Moreover, a State Party may not invoke the provisions of its internal law as justification for its failure to perform the Rome Statute.[7]

States Parties therefore have, in principle, no alternative to the Court's request for consistent cooperation. However, a requested State could base its refusal to cooperate notably on contrary regional law and the ground of protection of national security.[8] Regrettably, it can also be noted that there is no real possibility to sanction a State party's failure to cooperate.

The general obligation to cooperate has ramifications under the Rome Statute. The Statute presents several forms of cooperation, thus giving the obligation to cooperate several

---

and William A. SCHABAS (eds), *The Legislative History of the International Criminal Court*, 2nd ed., vol. 2, Leiden / Boston, Brill Nijhoff, 2016, pp. 730-36.

[4] Abdoul Aziz MBAYE and Sam Sasan SHOAMANESH, *ibid.*, p. 1792.

[5] MASSI LOMBAT, P.D., « Les sources et fondements de l'obligation de coopérer avec la Cour pénale internationale », *Quebec Journal of International Law*, vol. 27, No. 1, 2014, pp. 113-141 (spec. p. 114).

[6] DAVID, E., « La Cour pénale internationale », *RCADI*, 2005, II, vol. 313, pp. 325-454 (spec. p. 441).

[7] See Vienna Convention on the Law of Treaties, Art. 27.

[8] See *infra*.

dimensions. It was considered that the obligation of Article 86 did not cover the enforcement of sentences, in accordance with Part 10 of the Statute.[9] However, it is important to note that the general duty to cooperate extends to the enforcement of forfeiture measures and reparations orders issued by the Court. Seizures belong to the category of other forms of cooperation provided for in Article 93 of the Statute and, when ordering reparations in favour of the victims following a conviction, the Court may determine whether it is necessary, in order to give effect to the reparation orders, to request measures under Article 93-1 of the Statute.[10] The question this article aims to answer is: What is the legal basis for the obligation and refusal to cooperate of African States with the Court?

In the following paragraphs, the obligation to cooperate will be discussed, on the one hand, based on the relevant provisions of the Rome Statute and, on the other hand, this obligation can be created through *ad hoc* cooperation arrangements or agreements concluded by the Court and Non-Party States. The article also assesses the incorporation of the obligation to cooperate in eight African States Parties' laws. In addition, legal grounds for refusal of African States to cooperate with the Court will be discussed in relation to the *Al-Bashir* case.

1. Obligation of African States to Cooperate with the ICC

For a better understanding of the obligation of African States to cooperate (such obligation applies to all States Parties to the Rome Statute), it is necessary to research and analyse its legal bases. As long as the wait for a permanent

---

[9] PLÉNET,E., *Vers la création d'une prison internationale : l'exécution des peines prononcées par les juridictions pénales internationales*, Paris, L'Harmattan, 2010, pp. 295 *et seq.*

[10] ICC Statute, Art. 75(4).

international criminal court was, the result must nevertheless be put into perspective. Indeed, instead of a court benefiting from complete universality, a court with a universal vocation or a court with intermittent, hypothetical or even political universality has been created. In fact, as Robert Badinter pointed out, not without relevance, the only hypothesis in which the jurisdiction of the Court is universal is when a situation is referred to it the UN Security Council.[11] The universality of the Court, as seen in the context of the referral of the situations in Darfur and Libya, depends on the statement by the Security Council that third States must cooperate with the Court.[12]

The obligation to respect and ensure respect for international humanitarian law could be another source of the obligation to cooperate of states not party to the Rome Statute. In fact, an author noted that: 'States not party to the ICC are obliged to co-operate with it not only in instances of referrals by the UN Security Council but also under the provisions in the Geneva Conventions whereby states must 'respect and ensure respect' for international humanitarian law (IHL)".[13] It is not certain that the States concerned would easily embrace this idea. However, given that one of the objectives of the creation of the ICC is the suppression of serious violations of the Geneva Conventions of 1949, a state

---

11 BADINTER, R., « Avant-propos », in Julian FERNANDEZ and Xavier PACREAU (eds), *Statut de Rome de la Cour pénale internationale, Commentaire article par article, op. cit.*, pp. 9-11 (spec. p. 10); Jean-Baptiste JEANGÈNE VILMER, « Union africaine *versus* Cour pénale internationale : Répondre aux objections et sortir de la crise », *Revue Études Internationales,* vol. XLV, No. 1, March 2014, pp. 5-26 (spec. p. 5). This author believes that when a situation is referred to the ICC by the Security Council, all UN member states have an obligation to cooperate with it, which effectively makes its jurisdiction universal.

12 *Infra.*

13 WENQI, Z., « On co-operation by states not party to the International Criminal Court », *International Review of Red Cross*, vol. 88, No. 861, March 2006, pp. 87-110 (spec. p. 92).

not party to the Rome Statute, but a party to those conventions, may be obliged to respect and enforce those conventions in all circumstances. This requirement would include the obligation to cooperate with the ICC.[14]

All these hypotheses of linking third States to the Rome system suggest that all States should adapt their legal systems to the standards of international criminal justice. The fact that a State is a third party to the ICC does not absolutely close any possibility of cooperation, voluntary or compulsory, with the ICC. According to Hans-Peter Kaul, one of the first judges of the Court, third States are *de facto* part of the ICC system. This judge noted that:

> [t]his is particularly because the comprehensive codification of genocide, crimes against humanity and war crimes in articles 6, 7 and 8 of the Rome Statute has established value standards which are absolutely binding. It is generally recognized that also non-States Parties have to observe these standards and they have already recognized them - as is the case for example with the United States[15].

Without completely questioning Judge Kaul's analysis above, it must be admitted that a State may well incorporate the crimes of the Rome Statute into its criminal legislation without participating in practice in the suppression of these crimes. For instance, President Trump's National Security Adviser, John Bolton's vilification of the ICC raises serious

---

[14] *Ibid.*, p. 94.

[15] KAUL, H. P., "Kampala June 2010 – A First Review of the ICC Review Conference", *Goettingen Journal of International Law*, vol. 2, No. 2, 2010, pp. 649-667 (spec. p. 653). This author pointed that the ICC's jurisdiction may also have a great impact on non-States Parties notably because of two types of mechanisms, that is, "*firstly, in case of a referral of a situation by the Security Council of the UN, as it happened with regard to the situation in Darfur/Sudan by S/RES 1593, and secondly if nationals of non-States Parties commit international crimes* [...] *on the territory of a State Party. In this case, the ICC can have complementary jurisdiction according to the principle of territoriality laid down in Article 12(2)(a) of the Rome Statute.*"

doubts about the United States' willingness to comply with the relevant standards of the Rome Statute.[16]

It will simply be explained in the following paragraphs that, in accordance with the rules contained in the Vienna Convention on the Law of Treaties, the obligation to cooperate is based essentially on relevant statements of the Rome Statute. This treaty provides, however, for the possibility for non-Parties States to cooperate with the Court on the basis of *ad hoc* arrangements or agreements concluded between the Court and those States.

1.1. Obligation to Cooperate Based on the Rome Statute

At the outset, it should be noted that African States have an obligation to cooperate with the ICC under the Rome Statute. The scope of this duty to cooperate must be clarified. According to Eric David, the ICC can only assert a "customary obligation to cooperate" of third States.[17] That is why these non-States Parties are described as occasional partners of the Court. In accordance with the principle of relativity of the treaties, this obligation applies *a priori* only to States Parties to the Rome Statute. The latter are considered to be the principal subjects of this obligation, whereas the non-States Parties are only required to comply with it in certain circumstances.

1.1.1. An Obligation in Principle Borne by the States Parties Alone

The obligation to cooperate seems to lie solely with the States parties to the Rome Statute. The ICC is an independent

---

16 BOLTON, J., "*We will let the ICC die on its own. After all, for all intents and purposes, the ICC is already dead.*" 10 September 2018: Source: https://www.theguardian.com/us-news/2018/sep/10/john-bolton-castigate-icc-washington-speech (visited 10 August 2022).

17 DAVID, E., « La Cour pénale internationale », *op. cit.*, p. 360.

and autonomous international organisation with legal personality and the power to request the cooperation of States Parties. The latter have an obligation to cooperate not only in accordance with the provisions of the Rome Statute, but also in accordance with their respective laws.

The Rome Statute, like any treaty, is subject to all the legal rules applicable to treaties. As a result, it produces legal effects primarily with respect to States Parties. The latter are bound to implement it in good faith, without it being seen as a factor of loss of their sovereignty. The dominant voluntarist doctrine nevertheless considers that « *accepter d'être lié par la règle de droit* [...], *c'est surtout, quoi qu'on en dise, une limitation de souveraineté* ».[18]

In its first final judgment, the PCIJ "*decline*[d] *to see in the conclusion of any Treaty by which a State undertakes to perform or refrain from performing a particular act an abandonment of its sovereignty.* [...] *But the right of entering into international engagements is an attribute of State sovereignty.*"[19]

The fact of being a party to the Rome Statute does not therefore constitute a limitation of the sovereignty of the State, since it is considered that the principle of complementarity that coordinates the relations between the ICC and the States Parties is « *un moyen de légitimer la souveraineté judiciaire des États ayant un système judiciaire compétent, impartial et transparent* ».[20] This preservation of the sovereignty of States

---

[18] WEIL, P., « Le droit international en quête de son identité. Cours général de droit international public », RCADI, 1992, VI, vol. 237, pp. 9-370 (spec. p. 67). *Contra* : Alain PELLET thinks that « *ceci reflète la conception absolutiste et erronée de la souveraineté* ». See Alain PELLET, « Cours Général : Le droit international entre souveraineté et communauté internationale – La formation du droit international », *Anuário Brasileiro de Direito Internacional*, vol. II, 2007, pp. 12-74 (spec. p. 38).

[19] The *Wimbledon*, judgment of 17 August 1923, PCIJ, Ser. A, no. 1, p. 25.

[20] MASSI LOMBAT, P. D., « Les sources et fondements de l'obligation de coopérer avec la Cour pénale internationale », *op. cit.*, p. 117.

Parties does not exclude their obligation to incorporate the requirements of the Statute in their national legislation.

The effectiveness of the State cooperation could only be guaranteed where States Parties enact national legislation « *en prévoyant les mesures d'exécution nécessaires qui permettront d'éviter la multiplication des motifs de refus fondés sur le droit interne* »[21]. Indeed, compliance with this adaptation requirement is necessary in several cases as the guarantee of full cooperation with the Court.[22]

It should be noted that the obligation to cooperate remains with respect to the State Party withdrawing from the Statute, subject to certain conditions.[23] In fact, Article 127(2) of the Rome Statute provides:

> Its withdrawal shall not affect any cooperation with the Court in connection with criminal investigations and proceedings in relation to which the withdrawing State had a duty to cooperate and which were commenced prior to the date on which the withdrawal became effective, nor shall it prejudice in any way the continued consideration of any matter which was already under consideration by the Court prior to the date on which the withdrawal became effective.

To the question of what would happen if the crimes under the Rome Statute were committed during the phase in which a State was a party, but no proceeding was initiated before the withdrawal of the denouncing State took effect, Robert Kolb offered two answers.[24] First, and this is the most acceptable answer in this article, the author wrote that it is admissible to argue that article 127(2) constitutes a *lex specialis* and would be applicable only to the effects of denunciation of the Rome Statute. In this case, the conclusion is that the withdrawing

---

21 MBAYE, A. Z., and SHOAMANESH, S. S., « Article 86 », *ibid.*, p. 1794.
22 *Ibid.*
23 *Ibid.*, p. 1796.
24 KOLB, R., « Article 127 – Retrait », in Julian FERNANDEZ and Xavier PACREAU (eds), *Statut de Rome de la Cour pénale internationale. Commentaire article par article*, *op. cit.*, pp. 2213-2220 (spec. p. 2219).

State is not bound to cooperate with the Court.[25] Second, the author noted that:

> *il est possible de soutenir que le paragraphe 2 […] n'a pas pour but de déroger à l'ensemble du droit international général. Il ne serait alors pas limitatif. Dans ce cas, il serait possible d'appliquer analogiquement l'article 70 de la CVDT en affirmant que l'infraction pénale met en branle le Statut au moment de sa commission et que le retrait ne saurait porter atteinte à cette 'situation juridique des parties', c'est-à-dire à la compétence de la Cour à l'égard du crime et à l'égard des États concernés.*[26]

This second interpretation seems very broad, although some authors may prefer it to the previous one. This is particularly the case of Roger S. Clark for whom "[i]*t would seem to follow that if there were breaches of the substantive legal provisions of the Rome Statute on a State's territory or by its nationals prior to withdrawal, those offenses would still come within the jurisdiction of the Court even if the prosecution had not been commenced before withdrawal*".[27]

One cannot lose sight of the fact that the withdrawal of a State from the Rome Statute has, among other objectives, the exclusion of the ICC's jurisdiction over the territory of that State and its nationals. If cooperation between the States Parties and the Court is not easy, what about the cooperation that would unfold between a withdrawing State and the Court?

Based on the discussions above, it is clear that States Parties to the Rome Statute are primarily under the obligation to cooperate, but the Rome Statute provides for hypotheses of obligation relations between third States and the Court.

---

[25] *Ibid.*

[26] *Ibid.*

[27] CLARK, R. S., « Article 127 - Withdrawal », in Otto TRIFFTERER and Ambos KAI (eds), *Commentary on the Rome Statute of the International Criminal Court. Observers' Notes, Article by Article*, 3rd ed., Munich / Oxford / Baden-Baden, Nomos / Beck / Hart, 2016, pp. 2322-2324 (spec. p. 2324).

1.1.2. The Obligation to Cooperate of Third States Derived from Specific Provisions of the Rome Statute

The question of the ICC's jurisdiction over nationals of non-States Parties to the Rome Statute has always been one of the main grounds for disagreement or opposition from some major powers, notably the United States.[28] For this country, this question constitutes the essential imperfection of the Statute.[29] Non-States Parties to the Rome Statute (third States and signatories not ratifying) are not *de jure* recipients of the cooperation obligation of Article 86. By virtue of the principle of relativity or the relative effect of treaties (*pacta tertiis nec nocent nec prosunt*), these States are not, in principle, obliged to cooperate with the Court. This principle is part of the fundamental principles of treaty law. It was first recognized by international jurisprudence and by the practice

---

28 MEGRET, F., "Epilogue to an Endless Debate: The International Criminal Court's Third Party Jurisdiction and the Looming Revolution of International Law", *E.J.I.L.*, Vol. 12, n° 2, 2001, pp. 247-268 (spec. pp. 247-248); MAYERFELD, J., "The Democratic Legacy of the International Criminal Court", *The Fletcher Forum of World Affairs*, vol. 28, No. 2, 2004, pp. 147-156 (spec. pp. 147 and 153).

29 The United States ambassador David SCHEFFER has described the problem of the ICC's jurisdiction over the nationals of non-States Parties as the "single most problematic part of the Rome Treaty". See SCHEFFER, D., "International Criminal Court: The Challenge of Jurisdiction" (address at the annual meeting of the American Society of International Law on 26 March 1999), *Proceedings of the Annual Meeting (American Society of International Law)*, vol. 93, 1999, pp. 68-72 (spec. p. 69). *Contra*: MAYERFELD believes that, contrary to US criticism, the Court's jurisdiction over nationals of non-States Parties is not a violation of sovereignty or democracy. He points out that it supports sovereignty by helping countries defend themselves against the commission of atrocities on their territory by foreigners while States that authorise the ICC for this purpose fulfil a democratic obligation by ensuring the safety of their inhabitants. See Jamie MAYERFELD, *ibid.*, p. 153. See also Frédérique COULÉE, « Sur un État tiers bien peu discret : les États-Unis confrontés au Statut de la Cour pénale internationale », *AFDI*, vol. 49, 2003. pp. 32-70 (spec. p. 47).

of States, before being codified by the Vienna Conference on the Law of Treaties.

In its Judgment in the case concerning *Certain German Interests in Polish Upper Silesia*, the CPJI ruled that "[a] *treaty only creates law as between the States which are parties to it ; in case of doubt, no rights can be deduced from it in favour of third States.*"[30] The ICJ followed this position in its judgment in the case concerning the *aerial incident of 27 July 1955*, by stating that Article 36 § 5 of its Statute "*was without legal force so far as non-signatory States were concerned*".[31]

According to Article 34 of the Vienna Convention on the Law of Treaties 1969, "[a] *treaty does not create either obligations or rights for a third State without its consent.*" In accordance with this provision, in principle, non-States Parties to the Rome Statute may be required to cooperate with the ICC only under certain conditions and under certain circumstances. In fact, the Rome Statute contains specific provisions that offer the possibility of creating legal relations with non-party states. These are Articles 12(3) and 13(b).

1.1.2.1. In Case of Acceptance of the Jurisdiction of the Court (Article 12-3 of the Rome Statute)

The possibility given to States not party to the Statute to accept the jurisdiction of the Court[32] is part of a pragmatic approach towards these States.[33] The declaration by which the

30 *Certain German Interests in Polish Upper Silesia* (Germany v. Polish), judgment of 25 May 1926, PCIJ, Ser. A, no. 7, p. 29.

31 *Case concerning the Aerial Incident of July 27th, 1955* (Israel v. Bulgaria), Preliminary Objections, judgment of 26 May 1959, I.C.J. Reports 1959, p. 138.

32 The first part of Article 12(3) reads as follows: "*If the acceptance of a State which is not a Party to this Statute is required under paragraph 2, that State may, by declaration lodged with the Registrar, accept the exercise of jurisdiction by the Court with respect to the crime in question.*"

33 MASSI LOMBAT, P. D., « Les sources et fondements de l'obligation de coopérer avec la Cour pénale internationale », *op. cit.*, p. 119.

acceptance of the Court's jurisdiction is made "must be express, unequivocal, and precise as to the crime(s) or situation it applies to".[34] Such a declaration shall in principle be made by the executive power of the State and shall have the main effect of subjecting the third State concerned to the cooperation regime applicable to the States Parties. Indeed, the second sentence of Article 12(3) of the Rome Statute reads as follows: "*The accepting State shall cooperate with the Court without any delay or exception in accordance with Part 9.*" It is clear that the statements of acceptance of the Court's jurisdiction are in fact "more practical" than a legislative move to ratify the Statute.[35]

With respect to the scope of Article 12-3, it should be noted that « *il ne saurait être question pour un État non partie de soumettre, en tant que tel, une situation à la Cour, et de contraindre le procureur à ouvrir une enquête* »[36]. The declaration of recognition of the jurisdiction of the ICC does not have the effect of automatically triggering the exercise of that jurisdiction. In order for it to have such an effect, either the Prosecutor must have opened an investigation, in accordance with Article 15, or a situation must have been referred by a State Party, pursuant to Article 14 of the Statute.[37] While the declaration referred to in Article 12(3) must thus intervene to remove the

---

[34] BOURGON, S., « Jurisdiction *Ratione Loci* », in CASSESE, A., GAETA, P., and R. W. D. JONES (eds), *The Rome Statute of the International Criminal Court: A Commentary*, Oxford, OUP, 2002, pp.559-569 (spec. p. 563).

[35] MASSI LOMBAT, P.S., « Les sources et fondements de l'obligation de coopérer avec la Cour pénale internationale », *op. cit.*, p. 119.

[36] HAUPAIS, N., « Article 12 – Conditions préalables à l'exercice de la compétence », in FERNANDEZ, J., and PACREAU, X., (eds), *Statut de Rome de la Cour pénale internationale, Commentaire article par article, op. cit.*, pp. 581-606 (spec. p. 594).

[37] *Ibid.* See also Amady BA, « L'effet et l'exécution des décisions internationales », in *Internationalisation du droit, internationalisation de la Justice*, 3rd Congress of AHJUCAF, Supreme Court of Canada, Ottawa, 21-23 June 2010, pp. 37-59 (spec. p. 42).

legal obstacle to the establishment of the Court's jurisdiction, it does not mean that an investigation will necessarily be opened, as shown by the precedent of the very first declaration of this kind made by Côte d'Ivoire. This State accepted the jurisdiction of the ICC on 18 April 2003.[38] The declaration in question was later confirmed by the governments of Laurent Gbagbo and Alassane Ouattara on 14 December 2010 and 3 May 2011[39] respectively. However, it was only on 3 October 2011 that Pre-Trial Chamber III authorized the Prosecutor to open on his own initiative an investigation into the situation in Côte d'Ivoire, concerning crimes under the Court's jurisdiction allegedly committed since 28 November 2010, in the context of post-election violence, and crimes that could be committed in the future in the context of this situation. On 22 February 2012, the same Chamber extended the jurisdiction of the Court in respect of crimes committed on Ivorian territory or by Ivorians as of 19 September 2002.

Pre-Trial Chamber I was given the opportunity to provide an interpretation of the ICC's normative framework for declaring acceptance of the Court's jurisdiction. The Chamber stated that:

> while States may choose to consent or not to the jurisdiction of the Court through declarations provided for in article 12(3) of the Statute, the scope of such declarations is predetermined by the ICC legal

---

[38] See Statement of Recognition (by the then Ivorian Minister of Foreign Affairs, Mamadou Bamba) https://www.icc-cpi.int/NR/rdonlyres/FF9939C2-8E97-4463-934C-BC8F351BA013/279779/ICDE1.pdf (visited 27 August 2022). The Ivorian State agreed that the Court should exercise its jurisdiction for crimes committed on Ivorian territory as of 19 September 2002. See ICC, Press Release, ICC-CPI-20050215-91, ICC - Registrar confirms that the Republic of Côte d'Ivoire has accepted the jurisdiction of the Court, 15 February 2005, https://asp.icc-cpi.int/press-releases/press-releases-2005/registrar-confirms-that-the-republic-of-c-te-d-ivoire-has-accepted-the-juris (visited 27 August 2022).

[39] Côte d'Ivoire ratified the Rome Statute on 15 February 2013.

framework. Most notably rule 44 of the Rules explicitly limits the discretion of States in framing the situation that may be investigated by the Court. [...] Rule 44 of the Rules was adopted in order to ensure that States that chose to stay out of the treaty could not use the Court "opportunistically". Indeed, there were concerns that the wording of article 12 (3) of the Statute, and specifically the reference to the acceptance of jurisdiction "with respect to the crime in question", would allow the Court to be used as a political tool by States not party to the Statute who could selectively accept the exercise of jurisdiction in respect of certain crimes or certain parties to a conflict.[40]

Therefore, the declaration of Article 12(3) implies the acceptance of jurisdiction over the crimes referred to in Article 5 of the Statute committed in the context of a situation rather than individual crimes or specific incidents.[41] In the case of Côte d'Ivoire, the consent of the State concerned crimes committed on its territory and by its nationals.

The first Palestinian declaration seemed to be based on a slightly different logic.[42] On January 22, 2009, the Palestinian National Authority filed with the Registry of the Court a declaration under Article 12(3) for the purpose of identifying, prosecuting and bringing to trial the perpetrators and

---

[40] *The Prosecutor v. Laurent Koudou Gbagbo*, No. ICC-02/11-01/11-212, Decision on the 'Corrigendum of the challenge to the jurisdiction of the International Criminal Court on the basis of articles 12(3), 19(2), 21(3), 55 and 59 of the Rome Statute filed by the Defence for President Gbagbo (ICC-02/11-01/11-129)', 15 August 2012 (ICC, Pre-Trial Chamber I), para. 59.

[41] STAHN,C., M. EL ZEIDY, M., and OLÁSOLO, H., « The International Criminal Court's Ad Hoc Jurisdiction Revisited », *AJIL*, vol. 99, 2005, pp. 421-431 (spec. pp. 427-428). BASSIOUNI,M.C., went in the same direction by stating that: "*the Court could exercise its jurisdiction with respect to any crime referred to in Article 5 arising out of a "situation" which is referred to it. The adjustment that results from Rule 44 of the Rule of Procedure and Evidence seems to confirm this, with its reference to "situation". The term "situation" is used for referral to the Court by a state party or by the Security Council, pursuant to Article 13.*" See BASSIOUNI, M. C., *The Legislative History of the International Criminal Court: Introduction, Analysis and Integrated Text*, vol. I, New York, Transnational Publishers, 2005, pp 84-85.

[42] HAUPAIS, N., « Article 12 », *op. cit.*, p. 594.

accomplices of acts committed on Palestinian territory since July 1, 2002.[43] Later, on 1 January 2015, the Registrar of the Court received a second declaration[44] filed, pursuant to Article 12(3) of the Rome Statute, by the Palestinian government declaring its acceptance of the ICC's jurisdiction as of 13 June 2014. Based on this second declaration, the Prosecutor opened a preliminary examination of the situation in Palestine on 16 January 2015.[45] It is obvious that this is an exceptional situation, namely a territory subject to the joint authority of an occupation force (Israel) and an entity whose status as a State is not fully acquired under international law, and Israel is not a party to the Rome Statute. Nicolas Haupais therefore concludes that the territory concerned is potentially an unsusceptible place to be 'hit' by legal action.[46] This analysis does not seem to be supported by the evolution of legal relations between Palestine and the Court. Indeed, this "State" acceded to the Rome Statute on 2 January 2015[47] and

[43] Declaration by the Minister of Justice of the Palestinian National Authority of 21 January 2009, https://www.icc-cpi.int/sites/default/files/NR/rdonlyres/74EEE201-0FED-4481-95D4-C8071087102C/279837/20090122PalestinianDeclaration2FRA.pdf (visited 27 August 2022).

[44] See ICC, Press Release, ICC-CPI-20150105-PR1080 Palestine declares acceptance of ICC jurisdiction since 13 June 2014, 5 January 2015, https://www.icc-cpi.int/news/palestine-declares-acceptance-icc-jurisdiction-13-june-2014 (visited 27 August 2022). Declaration of the President of the State of Palestine, https://www.icc-cpi.int/sites/default/files/iccdocs/PIDS/press/Palestine_A_12-3.pdf (visited 27 August 2022).

[45] See ICC, Press Release, ICC-OTP-20150116-PR1083, The Prosecutor of the International Criminal Court, Fatou Bensouda, opens a preliminary examination of the situation in Palestine, 16 January 2015, https://www.icc-cpi.int/news/prosecutor-international-criminal-court-fatou-bensouda-opens-preliminary-examination-situation (visited 27 August 2022).

[46] HAUPAIS, N., « Article 12 », *op. cit.*, p. 596.

[47] On the list of States Parties to the Rome Statute on the website dedicated to the Collection of Treaties Registered with the UNSG one can

allowed the entry into force of the Kampala amendments on the crime of aggression by being the 30th State to ratify them.[48]

The declarations made by Ukraine follow the same logic as the first Palestinian declaration. Indeed, on 9 April 2014, the Embassy of Ukraine in the Netherlands had informed the Registrar of the ICC of the acceptance of the Court's jurisdiction, in accordance with Article 12(3) of the Rome Statute, for the purpose of identifying, to prosecute and try the perpetrators and accomplices of the criminal acts committed on Ukrainian territory in the period from 21 November 2013 to 22 February 2014.[49] This acceptance of jurisdiction is based on the declaration made by the Ukrainian *Verkhovna Rada* (Parliament) on 25 February 2014.[50] Following this declaration, the preliminary examination of the situation in Ukraine was announced on 25 April 2014. On 8 September 2015, the Registrar of the ICC was notified of a

---

read "State of Palestine" with the corresponding accession date (2 January 2015), https://treaties.un.org/Pages/ViewDetails.aspx?src=TREATY&mtdsg_no=XVIII-10&chapter=18&clang=_en (visited 7 September 2022).

48 See ICC, Press Release, State of Palestine becomes the thirtieth State to ratify the Kampala amendments on the crime of aggression, 29 June 2016, https://www.icc-cpi.int/news/state-palestine-becomes-thirtieth-state-ratify-kampala-amendments-crime-aggression (visited 7 September 2022).

49 These are crimes committed during the Maidan demonstrations, that is, before and during the fall of pro-Russian President Viktor Yanukovych. This limitation cannot be binding on the ICC Prosecutor. According to some commentators, "apart from providing a limited temporal jurisdiction, it seems that Ukraine has attempted to restrict the Court's *ratione materiae* and *ratione personae* jurisdiction." See SCHABAS W., A., and PECORELLA, G., "Article 12 - Preconditions to the exercise of jurisdiction", in TRIFFTERER, O., and AMBOS, K., (eds), *Commentary on the Rome Statute of International Criminal Court, Observer's notes, article by article*, 3rd ed., Munich / Oxford / Baden-Baden, Nomos / Beck / Hart, 2016, pp. 672-689 (spec. p. 688).

50 Declaration available on https://www.icc-cpi.int/itemsDocuments/997/declarationRecognitionJuristiction09-04-2014.pdf (visited 7 September 2022).

second declaration made by the Ukrainian Parliament on 4 February 2015.[51] As in the first declaration, Ukraine accepted the jurisdiction of the Court in this second declaration with the aim of identifying, prosecuting and bringing to trial the perpetrators and accomplices of the crimes committed in its territory from 20 February 2014 onwards.

Moreover, an act of acceptance of the Court's jurisdiction gives rise to an obligation of cooperation on the part of a non-Party State equal to that of a State Party. In the notifications of its two declarations, Ukraine thus undertook to cooperate with the Court without delay or exception, under Part 9 of the Rome Statute. As regards the declaration of Article 12(3), it is a unilateral act of the State, the legal scope of which is clear in international law. Despite their absence from the provision of Article 38 of the Vienna Convention on the Law of Treaties, the existence of acts by which a State, acting alone, expresses its will, and which produce effects in international law, is indisputable.[52] If engaging in the process of recognition of the Court's jurisdiction is voluntary, as long as the State concerned accepts it, it is subject to an obligation to cooperate similar to that of the States Parties. In fact, as per Article 12(3) of the Rome Statute, "there does not seem to be any consequence should an accepting State fail to cooperate as required."[53] It should be recalled, however, that the

[51] Declaration available on https://www.icc-cpi.int/iccdocs/other/Ukraine_Art_12-3_declaration_08092015.pdf (visited 7 September 2022).

[52] DAILLIER, P., FORTEAU, M., and PELLET, A., *Droit international public*, 8th ed., Paris, LGDJ/Lextenso, 2009, p. 395. See also *Legal Status of Eastern Greenland* (Denmark v. Norway), judgment of 5 April 1933, ser. A/B, no. 53, p. 69; *Nuclear Tests* (New Zealand v. France), judgment of 20 December 1974, I.C.J. Reports 197, pp. 268 *et seq.*

[53] SCHABAS, W .A., and PECORELLA, G., "Article 12 - Preconditions to the exercise of jurisdiction", TRIFFTERER, O., and AMBOS, K., (eds), *Commentary on the Rome Statute of International Criminal Court, Observer's notes, article by article, op. cit.*, pp. 672-689 (spec. p. 684). See also *The Prosecutor v. Simone Gbagbo*, ICC-02/11-01/12-47-Red, Decision on Côte d'Ivoire's

ratification of the Statute and the accession to it respectively by Côte d'Ivoire and Palestine, have rendered superseded their declarations of recognition of the competence of the Court.

2.1.2.2. In Case of Referral of a Situation to the Prosecutor by the United Nations Security Council (Article 13(b) of the Rome Statute)

The possibility for the United Nations Security Council to refer situations to the ICC[54], on the one hand, and the hypothesis of international crimes (falling within the jurisdiction of the Court) committed by nationals of States not parties in the territory of States Parties, on the other hand, constitute legal elements of connecting non-States Parties to the ICC system.[55] Article 13(b) allows the ICC to exercise its jurisdiction if "[a] *situation in which one or more of such crimes appears to have been committed is referred to the Prosecutor by the Security Council acting under Chapter VII of the Charter of the United Nations*". This type of referral constitutes the only hypothesis in which the system of preconditions laid down in Article 12 of the Statute does not apply. The Security Council is in fact the only entity capable of activating the jurisdiction of the ICC regardless of any connection relating to the territorial State or the nationality of the suspect and the crime.[56] However, this power, when exercised, does not make it possible to

---

challenge to the admissibility of the case against Simone Gbagbo, 11 December 2014 (ICC, Pre-Trial Chamber I) where the Chamber recalled Côte d'Ivoire's obligation to surrender Simone Gbagbo to Court.

54 For relevant provisions on the relations between the ICC and the UN Security Council, see notably Article 1, Article 13, Article 12 (1), (2), (3); Articles 13 to 15, Article 17 of the Rome Statute.

55 KAUL, H. P., « Kampala June 2010 – A First Review of the ICC Review Conference », *op. cit.*, p. 653.

56 MASSI LOMBAT, P., D., « Les sources et fondements de l'obligation de coopérer avec la Cour pénale internationale », *op. cit.*, p. 118. See also DELLA MORTE, G., « Les frontières de la compétence de la Cour pénale internationale : observations critiques », *RIDP*, vol. 73, 2002, pp. 23-57 (spec. p. 44).

automatically activate the obligation to cooperate of non-States Parties to the Rome Statute. One can therefore only partially subscribe to Eric David's position that « [l]*es Etats non parties peuvent être tenus de coopérer avec la Cour dans deux autres hypothèses : soit sur demande expresse du Conseil de sécurité, soit, logiquement, en cas de saisine de la Cour par le Conseil de sécurité* »[57]. Indeed, the first hypothesis mentioned is indisputable, but the second is less so. It is true that article 25 of the Charter of the United Nations makes all Security Council decisions binding on all UN member states. However, if it is certain that these States are obliged to implement the measures adopted by the Security Council,

> [i]l s'entend que le respect de cette hiérarchie est soumis à la condition de licéité des mesures prescrites. En principe, le non-respect du droit international par le Conseil affranchit l'État et toute entité destinataire de mesures de cet organe principal des Nations Unies de l'obligation de les mettre en œuvre[58].

This position is easily followed, since Article 10 of the Rome Statute states that: "*Nothing in* [Part 2 on Jurisdiction, Admissibility and Applicable Law] *shall be interpreted as limiting or prejudicing in any way existing or developing rules of international law for purposes other than this Statute.*" Nicolas Angelet listed three principles of international law that generally limit the action of the Security Council. These are the principle of proportionality, the requirement to respect the purposes and principles of the United Nations, and the prohibition of the settlement of international disputes by force.[59]

---

[57] DAVID, E., *La Cour pénale internationale*, *op. cit.*, pp. 360 et 440-441.

[58] MOUANGUE KOBILA, J., « L'Afrique et les juridictions internationales pénales », *Cahiers Thucydide*, No. 10, Paris, Centre Thucydide of the University of Paris 2, Panthéon Assas - Analyse et recherche en Relations internationales, pp. 47-48. See also ANGELET, N., "Protest against Security Council Decisions", in WELLENS, K., (ed.), *International Law Theory and Practice. Essays in Honour of Eric SUY*, The Hague / Boston / London, Martinus Nijhoff, 1998, pp. 277-285.

[59] ANGELET, N., "International Law Limits to the Security Council", in

Since the Court was not created by the Security Council, it does not benefit from the effect of Article 103 of the Charter of the United Nations.[60] The situation would not be entirely different when the Court is seized by the Security Council in accordance with Article 13(b) of the Statute. Indeed, even if the States, Parties or not to the Rome Statute, are almost all members of the United Nations, when the Security Council refers a situation to the Court for investigation and prosecution, this does not *a priori* involve all members of the United Nations. Some authors contest the fact that all UN member states, whether parties to the Rome Statute or not, are required to cooperate in the event of a referral of a situation to the ICC by the Security Council.[61]

Eric David[62] explains that the decisions of the ICC, when it is seized by the Security Council, do not automatically become similar to the decisions of the Security Council on cooperation; third States to the Rome Statute are therefore not *a priori* obliged to respond to them; for it to be otherwise,

---

GOWLLAND-DEBBAS, V., (ed.), *United Nations Sanctions and International Law*, The Hague / London / Boston, Kluwer Law International, 2001, pp. 71-82 (spec., pp. 72-81) [cited by MOUANGUE KOBILA, J., *ibid.*, p. 48, note 229].

60 CAZALA, J., « Article 89 - Remise de certaines personnes à la Cour », in FERNANDEZ, J., and PACREAU, X., (eds), *Statut de Rome de la Cour pénale internationale, Commentaire article par article, op. cit.*, pp. 1835-1847 (spec. p. 1840).

61 MOUANGUE KOBILA, J., « L'Afrique et les juridictions internationales pénales », *op. cit.*, p. 48 ; FAŁKOWSKA, M., and VERDEBOUT, A., « L'opposition de l'Union africaine aux poursuites contre Omar Al Bashir : Analyse des arguments juridiques avancés pour entraver le travail de la Cour pénale internationale et leur expression sur le terrain de la coopération », *Revue Belge de Droit International,* vol. XLV, No. 1, 2012, pp. 201-236 (spec. p. 234). *Contra*: According to WENQI,Z., the referral of a situation to the Court by the Security Council implies an obligation to cooperate of both States Parties and non-States Parties to the Rome Statute. See Zhu WENQI, "On co-operation by states not party to the International Criminal Court", *op. cit.*, p. 91.

62 DAVID, E., *La Cour pénale internationale*, *op. cit.*, p. 367.

the Security Council, in referring the situation to the Court, must decide that third States must provide assistance to the Court, as in the case of Darfur[63], and that of Libya[64]. The Security Council's request should be in accordance with international law, otherwise the requested State may and must ignore it.[65]

1.2. The Obligation to Cooperate Based on ad hoc Cooperation Arrangements or Agreements

The scope of the cooperation arrangements or arrangements in question appears to be "less vertical"[66] when one looks at the process of conclusion of such arrangements or agreements, even if the cooperation mechanisms they establish are similar to those provided for in the Rome Statute.

1.2.1. Conclusion of *ad hoc* Cooperation Arrangements or Agreements between the Court and Non-Party States

Ad hoc cooperation arrangements or agreements between the ICC and non-Parties States to its Statute are necessary in order to create an obligation (to cooperate) relationship between the Court and those States. However, the Court may only "invite"

63 UN Doc S/RES/1593 (2005) of 31 March 2005, para 2: The Security Council "decide[d] *that the Government of Sudan and all other parties to the conflict in Darfur, shall cooperate fully with and provide any necessary assistance to the Court and the Prosecutor pursuant to this resolution and, while recognizing that States not party to the Rome Statute have no obligation under the Statute, urges all States and concerned regional and other international organizations to cooperate fully.*"

64 UN.Doc.S/RES/1970 (2011) of 26 February 2011, para. 5: The Security Council "decide[d] *that the Libyan authorities shall cooperate fully with and provide any necessary assistance to the Court and the Prosecutor pursuant to this resolution and, while recognizing that States not party to the Rome Statute have no obligation under the Statute, urges all States and concerned regional and other international organizations to cooperate fully with the Court and the Prosecutor.*"

65 KOBILA, M., J., « L'Afrique et les juridictions internationales pénales », *op. cit.*, p. 48.

66 MASSI LOMBAT, P. D., « Les sources et fondements de l'obligation de coopérer avec la Cour pénale internationale », *op. cit.*, p. 121.

third States to provide assistance under Part 9 of the Rome Statute "*on the basis of an* ad hoc *arrangement, an agreement with such State or any other appropriate basis*".[67] Zhu Wenqi noted that the word "invite" in Article 87(5)(a) "shows that co-operation by non-party states with the ICC is in the legal category of co-operation of a 'voluntary nature' alone"[68], as evidenced by the practice of several African and non-African States.

It should, however, be noted that voluntarism should be sought in the conclusion of the cooperation arrangement or agreement and not in the main effect resulting from it, namely the obligation to cooperate. In fact, as noted by Olympia Bekou and Robert Cryer, "[t]he State concerned possesses a degree of flexibility to decide the type, field and length of cooperation to be provided to the Court".[69] These authors pointed out that this flexibility could be problematic for the Court, which, bound by its Statute, will not be inclined to go beyond it to accommodate the wishes of a third State.[70] In such a situation, the Court may face a dilemma. It must either refuse the assistance of a State or accept the conditions and the limit that that State intends to place on its assistance.[71]

In the absence of details in the Rome Statute on the ways for concluding *ad hoc* cooperation arrangements or agreements, it may be concluded that they are left to the

---

67 Article 87(5)(a) of the Rome Statute. According to WENQI, the words "*or any other appropriate basis*" in this article mean that the ways and means of cooperation by States not party to the Statute "are quite flexible." See Zhu WENQI, « On co-operation by states not party to the International Criminal Court », *op. cit.*, p. 109.

68 WENQI, Z., *ibid.*, p. 89. See also BEKOU, O., and CRYER, R.,"The International Criminal Court and Universal Jurisdiction: A Close Encounter?", *International and Comparative Law Quarterly*, vol. 56, No. 1, January 2007, pp. 49-68 (spec. p. 62).

69 BEKOU, O., and CRYER, R., *ibid.*

70 *Ibid.*

71 SLUITER, G., "The Surrender of War Criminals to the International Criminal Court", *Loyola of Los Angeles International and Comparative Law Review*, vol. 25, 2003, pp. 605-652 (spec. p. 610).

discretion of the Court and the States concerned.[72] Prior acceptance of the Court's jurisdiction is not necessary in the context of cooperation on the basis of an *ad hoc* arrangement or agreement referred to in Article 87(5)(a). What is certain is that when an *ad hoc* arrangement concerning the investigation or prosecution of one or more specific crimes or a more general cooperation agreement is concluded with a non-party State, the latter is obliged to cooperate with the Court.[73] The scope of the obligation to cooperate, however, depends on the content of the *ad hoc* arrangement or agreement. In fact,

> [b]y including in the Statute the provision at issue, States Parties have indeed decided to bind themselves reciprocally to grant the Court, as their common organ, the power to carry out not only an internal state activity, of a judicial nature, but also an external state activity, concerning the conclusion of agreements of cooperation and judicial assistance with States which are not parties to the Statute. These agreements are to be reached by the Court on behalf of the States parties to the Statute, which are thus the subjects entitled to request the implementation of such arrangements.[74]

Although it is clear that *ad hoc* cooperation arrangements or agreements between the Court and third States are subject to the law of the treaties, concern remains, however, as to the exact meaning of certain concepts contained in Article 87-5-a). These include the terms "*ad hoc* arrangement" and "any other appropriate basis". With respect to the *ad hoc* arrangement, Massi Lombat believes it can be verbal or written.[75] It is easy to follow the author when he specifies that

---

[72] MASSI LOMBAT, P. D., « Les sources et fondements de l'obligation de coopérer avec la Cour pénale internationale », *op. cit.*, p. 122.

[73] CIAMPI, A., « Article 87. Demandes de coopération : Dispositions générales », in FERNANDEZ, J., and PACREAU, X., (eds), *Statut de Rome de la Cour pénale internationale, Commentaire article par article, op. cit.*, pp. 1805-1820 (spec. p. 1813).

[74] PALMISANO, G., "The ICC and Third States », in SCHABAS, W. A., and LATTANZI, F., (eds), *Essays on the Rome Statute of the ICC*, Il Sirente, Fagnano Alto, 1999, pp. 391-425 (spec. p. 391).

[75] MASSI LOMBAT, P. D., « Les sources et fondements de l'obligation de coopérer avec la Cour pénale internationale », *op. cit.*, p. 123.

the verbal nature of an *ad hoc* arrangement concluded between the Court and the non-party State does not prevent the international responsibility of that State in the event of a breach of the arrangement. Indeed, in the case concerning the *Legal Status of Eastern Greenland*, the PCIJ ruled that the verbal commitment made by the Norwegian Minister of Foreign Affairs, Ihlen (*Ihlen Declaration*) to the Danish Ambassador in 1919, bound Norway in all circumstances, even if a formal treaty had not been concluded.[76]

The words "any other appropriate basis" may refer to whether to a Security Council[77] resolution or to international custom in accordance with Article 38 of the Vienna Convention on the Law of Treaties.[78] As per this article, "[n]*othing in articles 34 to 37 precludes a rule set forth in a treaty from becoming binding upon a third State as a customary rule of international law, recognized as such.*"

Ad hoc cooperation arrangements or agreements, where they define a general framework for cooperation on matters falling within the competence of more than one organ of the Court, shall be negotiated under the authority of the President of the Court, which may ask the Advisory Committee on Legal Texts to make recommendations to it.[79] However, the existence of such an agreement, that is, on the general framework for cooperation and involving the jurisdiction of more than one organ of the Court, does not prevent the Prosecutor from concluding agreements referred to in Article

---

76 *Legal Status of Eastern Greenland* (Denmark v. Norway), *op. cit.*

77 It is recognized that a Security Council resolution acting under Chapter VII of the UN Charter may constitute the "appropriate basis" for the obligation of third States to cooperate with the Court (provided that such resolution complies with international law). See Annalisa CIAMPI, « Article 87 », *op. cit.*, p. 1814. See also Pierrot Damien MASSI LOMBAT, « Les sources et fondements de l'obligation de coopérer avec la Cour pénale internationale », *op. cit.*, p. 123.

78 MASSI LOMBAT, P. D., *ibid.*

79 ICC Regulations, Regulation 107(1).

54(3)(d) of the Statute. As per this provision, the Prosecutor may "[e]*nter into such arrangements or agreements, not inconsistent with this Statute, as may be necessary to facilitate the cooperation of a State, intergovernmental organization or person*". However, the Prosecutor must inform the Presidency of his intention to do so, unless there are confidentiality related reasons that do not permit it.[80] In the case of Article 54(3)(d), third States are no longer the only ones concerned. Such arrangements or agreements may be concluded between the Prosecutor and the States Parties. Indeed, the pursuit of enhanced cooperation may prompt the Prosecutor to negotiate and conclude such agreements with States Parties.

The *ad hoc* cooperation arrangement or agreement concluded between the Court and the third State constitutes the source of the latter's obligation to cooperate. However, in order to harmonize the relations of the Court with the States, the content of such agreements must largely be based on the provisions of the Rome Statute and the Rules of Procedure and Evidence of the Court.[81]

1.2.2. Obligation to Cooperate of Third States under *ad hoc* Arrangements or Agreements

To date, the ICC has concluded agreements or arrangements with States on various aspects of cooperation and assistance. In principle, the cooperation regime as provided for by the Rome Statute and the obligation to implement national procedures should be sufficient to ensure the effectiveness of the Court. In practice, however, Part 9 of the Statute may be regarded as defining the general obligations of States Parties. This is why the Statute provides for the possibility to conclude special voluntary cooperation agreements when it comes to specific forms of cooperation.[82]

---

80 *Ibid.*, Regulation 107(2).

81 MASSI LOMBAT, P. D., « Les sources et fondements de l'obligation de coopérer avec la Cour pénale internationale », *op. cit.*, p. 122.

82 Article 54(3)(d) of the Rome Statute.

It is obvious that third States are not the ones with whom the Prosecutor may conclude such cooperation agreements. For instance, the cooperation laws of South Africa[83] and Mauritius[84] provide for the possibility to conclude special cooperation agreements with the Court. In practice, this was also demonstrated by the conclusion of judicial cooperation agreements between the Office of the Prosecutor and the Democratic Republic of Congo and Uganda, two States Parties to the Rome Statute, respectively in October and September 2004. While the main objective of these agreements was to get a cooperation more strengthened than that referred to in Part 9 of the Statute, it should be pointed out that their conclusion was intended to counterbalance the absence, at the time, of a national legislation on cooperation and the non-ratification of the Agreement on the Privileges and Immunities of the Court.[85] On 12 October 2004, an Interim Memorandum of Understanding was signed between the Court and the DRC to facilitate the independence, security and confidentiality of the Court's activities on the ground. This instrument was to remain in force until the Congolese authorities ratified the Agreement on the Privileges and Immunities of the Court. It is worth recalling that the DRC acceded to the Agreement only on 3 July 2007, while Uganda ratified it on 21 January 2009.[86]

Voluntary cooperation with the Court can also be formalised through an *ad hoc* arrangement. An illustration was

---

[83] Section 33 of Implementation of the Rome Statute of the International Criminal Court Act 2002.

[84] Section 40 of International Criminal Court Act 2011.

[85] UBÉDA-SAILLARD, M., « L'obligation de coopérer avec les juridictions internationales », in ASCENSIO, H., DECAUX, E., and PELLET, A., (eds), *Droit international pénal*, 2nd ed., Paris, Pedone, 2000, pp. 1137-1157 (p. 1141).

[86] Source : https://treaties.un.org/Pages/ViewDetails.aspx?src=TREATY&mtdsg_no=XVIII-13&chapter=18&clang=_fr (visited 5 September 2022).

offered in the context of the situation in Georgia. If this State is party to the Rome Statute - since September 5, 2003 - it is not the case for Russia, which signed it on 13 September 2000, before withdrawing its signature on 30 November 2016.[87] The Court proposed to help Russia open investigations and prosecute persons suspected of having committed crimes during the armed conflict in South Ossetia[88] that began on the night of 7-8 August 2008. At that time, Russia undertook to cooperate fully with the Court to ensure that all victims of the crimes were given justice.[89] Subsequently, on 27 August 2008, the Prosecutor asked the Russian and Georgian governments to provide him with some information, which they both did. Russia had even fulfilled its commitment to the Court by sending 3817 submissions to the OTP.[90]

In addition, the Registry of the Court has concluded several agreements with States on the protection and resettlement of witnesses. However, for security reasons, it was felt that such agreements could not be made public. On 21 November 2016, during the signing of a Cooperation Agreement on Witness Protection between Argentina and the Court, the Registrar indicated that this signing increased the number of cooperation agreements in this area to 18.[91]

---

87 C.N.886.2016.TREATIES-XVIII.10 (Depositary Notification), Russian Federation: Communication, 30 November 2016 https://treaties.un.org/doc/Publication/CN/2016/CN.886.2016-Eng.pdf (visited 5 September 2022).

88 MASSI LOMBAT, P. D., « Les sources et fondements de l'obligation de coopérer avec la Cour pénale internationale », *op. cit.*, p. 124.

89 See ICC, Press Release, ICC-OTP-20100310-PR505, ICC Prosecutor is working with the Russian Federation to promote justice for all victims of Georgian conflict - OTP and Russian Federation pledge co-operation at conclusion of Moscow visit, 10 March 2010, https://www.icc-cpi.int/news/icc-prosecutor-working-russian-federation-promote-justice-all-victims-georgian-conflict-otp (visited 9 September 2022).

90 Amady, B., A., « L'effet et l'exécution des décisions internationales », *op. cit.*, p. 45.

91 See ICC, Press Release, ICC-CPI-20161122-PR1258, Argentina and

It is not enough for a State to ratify the Statute or to pass a law of cooperation with the Court. Certain aspects of the Court's activities require the signing of special agreements, in order to promote stronger and more operational cooperation relationships with the ICC. In practice, it is considered that the signing of such specific agreements can lead States to cooperate more effectively. If the conclusion of a special cooperation agreement with the Court imposes on the State an obligation of cooperation similar to that, more generally, resulting from the Statute, the specificity of the field of cooperation is such as to facilitate the execution of the former.

2. Incorporation of the Obligation to Cooperate in African States Parties' Laws

African States Parties' laws on cooperation with the ICC confirm by their existence the obligation to cooperate of the States concerned. They aim at enabling those States to fulfil their obligation to cooperate with the Court. These are the laws of the following States: Burkina Faso[92], Central African

International Criminal Court sign an agreement on Witnesses' protection, 22 November 2016, https://www.icc-cpi.int/news/argentina-and-international-criminal-court-sign-agreement-witnesses-protection (visited 9 September 2022).

[92] Law No. 052-2009/AN Determining Jurisdiction and Procedure for the Implementation of the Rome Statute of the International Criminal Court by the Burkinabe Courts, 3 December 2009 (promulgated by Decree No. 2009-894/PRES, 31 December 2009) (hereafter 'Burkina Faso ICC Law').

Republic[93], Democratic Republic of Congo[94], Kenya[95], Mauritius[96], Uganda[97], South Africa[98], and the Union of the Comoros[99]. On the one hand, there are laws that do not expressly incorporate the provision of Article 86 of the Statute and, on the other hand, there are those, which either reproduce it or take them up again, specifying the mandatory nature of the obligation to cooperate. This legislative diversity with respect to the mandatory nature of the obligation to cooperate confirms the Court's lack of coercive power vis-à-vis States.

2.1. The Diversity of African Laws as regards the Imperative Nature of the General Obligation to Cooperate

African States laws vary with respect to the incorporation of the general obligation to cooperate as provided for by Article 86 of the Rome Statute. Most of these laws, like the

---

93 Law No. 10.002 of 06 January 2010 on the Criminal Procedure Code (hereafter 'Central African Republic CPC'). Title XIV of Book III of this Code is entitled 'Cooperation with the International Criminal Court' (Arts. 344 to 363).

94 Law No 15/024 of 31 December 2015 Amending and Supplementing Decree of 6 August 1959 on the Criminal Procedure Code (hereafter 'Democratic Republic of Congo CPC'). This law includes in Chapter II of Decree of 6 August 1959 on the Criminal Procedure Code as amended and supplemented by Law No 06/19, 20 July 2006, Section III *bis* entitled 'Cooperation with the International Criminal Court.'

95 The International Crimes Act 2008, 12 December 2008 (hereafter 'Kenya ICC Law').

96 International Criminal Court Act 2011 (Act No. 27), 26 July 2011 (hereafter 'Mauritius ICC Law').

97 The International Criminal Court Act 2010, 25 May 2010 (hereafter 'Uganda ICC Law').

98 Implementation of the Rome Statute of the International Criminal Court Act 2002 (Act 27), 12 July 2002 (hereafter 'South Africa ICC Law').

99 Law No. 11-022/AU 13 December 2011 on the Implementation of the Rome State (promulgated by Decree No. 12-022/PR, 04 February 2012) (hereafter 'Comoros ICC Law').

Rome Statute, emphasise on the imperative nature of the general obligation to cooperate of the States Parties. As Hans Kelsen pointed out, « *dans une règle de droit, la relation entre la condition et la conséquence est exprimée par le mot 'doit' pour bien marquer qu'une règle de droit n'a pas la même signification qu'une loi naturelle* ».[100]

An examination of the cooperation laws of the African States reveals a heterogeneity between them, particularly as regards the incorporation of Article 86 of the Rome Statute. In this connection, these laws can be classified into three main categories.

First of all, there are laws which, expressly referring to either Article 86 or the Statute, substantially incorporate the content of this article. This is the case with the legislation of the Union of the Comoros, Article 31 of which provides that: "*In accordance with Article 86 of the Statute, the Union of the Comoros shall cooperate fully with the Court in the investigation and prosecution of crimes within its jurisdiction.*" The same is true of the legislation of Burkina Faso, article 29-1 of which states that this State "*shall cooperate fully with the International Criminal Court in the investigation and prosecution of crimes within its jurisdiction, in accordance with the Rome Statute, the procedures provided for in this Act and other national provisions*". Article 21 *bis* of the DRC Cooperation Law provides that "*for the application of the Statute* [...], *the Democratic Republic of the Congo shall participate in the repression and cooperate fully with the Court in the investigation and prosecution it conducts for crimes within its jurisdiction.*" The Burkinabe, Comorian and Congolese laws therefore clearly specify the imperative nature of the obligation to cooperate through a satisfactory incorporation of Article 86 of the Rome Statute.

---

[100] KELSEN, H., « Théorie du droit international public », *RCADI*, 1953-III, vol. 84, pp. 1-203 (spec. p. 16).

Secondly, there are laws, which not only refer to the Statute but also above all contain a less satisfactory formulation of the general obligation to cooperate than those of the three laws mentioned above. This is the case in particular of the Criminal Procedure Code of the Central African Republic which refers to the Rome Statute without, however, repeating the terms of its Article 86 nor mentioning the term "fully" that underlines the imperative nature of the obligation to cooperate with the Court. Article 344-1 of this Code provides that "*in application of the Rome Statute* [...], *the Central African Republic shall participate in the repression of offences and cooperate with th*[e] *Court under the conditions set out in this Title*". This is also the case with South African legislation, article 14 of which provides that: "*The relevant competent authorities in the Republic must, subject to the domestic law of the Republic and the Statute, cooperate with, and render assistance to, the Court in relation to investigations and prosecutions* [...]." The Mauritian legislation has a similar wording. Its Article 21(1) states: "*The State shall, subject to any other enactment and the Statute, co-operate with, and render assistance to, the International Criminal Court in relation to investigations and prosecutions* [...]." As a result, Central African, Mauritian and South African laws are less clear on the imperative nature of the general obligation to cooperate. However, the absence of the term "fully", even if it makes these texts less emphatic (as compared to the Rome Statute), does not completely take away from the obligation to cooperate its imperative character in the said laws. Indeed, the reference made to the Statute by these laws certainly means that the obligation to cooperate of the States concerned will be fulfilled in accordance with the letter and spirit of the Statute. In addition, the words "shall ... cooperate" and "must ... cooperate" used by the Central African, Mauritian laws and South African laws respectively refer to the same thing, that is, the obligation to cooperate. It is important to note, however, that in the practice of some Anglo-Saxon States, the modal verbs "must" and "shall" indicate an obligation of result. In fact, Laurent Fabius, former Minister of Foreign Affairs of France, explained how at the COP 21 or CMP 11[101], a material error, having transformed in the English version of the Paris Agreement a "should" into a "shall", had to be corrected at the last moment in order to avoid a rejection by the American delegation, and thus the failure of that agreement.[102]

Finally, there are laws which do not expressly incorporate the provision of Article 86 of the Rome Statute. This includes the Senegalese law, which contains no provision on the general obligation to cooperate. However, in the second paragraph of the explanatory statement of this law reads as follows: "*In order to allow full cooperation in investigation and prosecution, the crimes of the Rome Statute are incorporated in the Penal Code...*" This means that, despite the silence of the operative part of the law on this obligation, Senegal intends to cooperate fully with the Court. The Kenyan and Ugandan laws also do not contain specific provisions on the general duty to cooperate. However, these laws make repeated references to the Statute and the Kenyan law contains, in appendix, the said Statute, which allows concluding that the States concerned incorporate the provisions of the Rome Statute relating to cooperation as a whole.

The diversity of African States' cooperation laws with respect to the incorporation of the general obligation to cooperate highlights the ICC's inability to issue orders to State authorities with respect to cooperation. Its requests for cooperation do not constitute absolute orders, the Court

---

101 The 2015 United Nations Climate Change Conference, COP 21 or CMP 11, held in Paris, France, from 30 November to 12 December 2015. It was the 21st yearly session of the Conference of the Parties (COP) to the 1992 United Nations Framework Convention on Climate Change (UNFCCC) and the 11th session of the Meeting of the Parties (CMP) to the 1997 Kyoto Protocol.

102 FABIUS, L., *37 Quai d'Orsay. Diplomatie française 2012-2016*, Paris, Plon, 2016, Chapiter 1 (epup).

having no power of coercion over the requested States Parties.

2.2. The Lack of Coercive Power of the ICC against States in Cooperation Matters

According to Ubéda-Saillard, the obligation to cooperate is not full and complete since « *d'une part, une certaine liberté, qui transparaît en général dans le contenu des lois de mise en œuvre, est laissée à l'État quant au choix des moyens et, d'autre part, on ne saurait prétendre qu'un résultat est exigé obligatoirement* »[103]. Indeed, it goes without saying that the Court's requests for cooperation are not accompanied by any real power of compulsion.[104] The ICC is nevertheless entitled to make a finding on the failure of the State having the obligation to cooperate with it and refer it to the Assembly of States Parties (ASP) or, where the Security Council referred the situation to the Court, to the Security Council.[105] Nevertheless, the relevant ICC legal instruments do not specify the outcome of the Court's referral of the refusal to cooperate. From these texts, there is no indication of the content of the measures that may be taken by the ASP to encourage a return to cooperation or to draw the consequences of a persistent refusal by a State.[106]

---

103 UBÉDA-SAILLARD, M., « L'obligation de coopérer avec les juridictions internationales », in ASCENSIO, H., DECAUX, E., and PELLET, A., (eds), *Droit international pénal*, 1st ed., Paris, Pedone, 2000, pp. 951-967 (spec. p. 954).

104 ITSOUHOU MBADINGA, M., « Variations des rapports entre les juridictions pénales internationales et les juridictions nationales dans la répression des crimes internationaux », *Revue Trimestrielle des Droits de l'Homme*, vol. 56, 2003, pp. 1221-1246 (spec. p. 1230).

105 Article 87(7) of the Rome Statute. Regulation 109(3) states that: "*Before making a finding in accordance with article 87, paragraph 7, the Chamber shall hear from the requested State.*"

106 See Serge SUR, « Vers une Cour pénale internationale : la Convention de Rome entre les O.N.G et le Conseil de sécurité », *RGDIP*, vol. 103, no. 1, 1999, pp. 29-45 (spec. p. 43). See also Olympia BEKOU and CRYER, R., "The International Criminal Court and Universal Jurisdiction: A Close

In the light of the provisions of the Statute, the ASP has no power to sanction a defaulting State. It is worth recalling that the Court had to inform the ASP and the Security Council of the lack of cooperation of some States Parties in the context of the situation in Darfur. These include Chad, Djibouti, Malawi and Uganda.[107] Since Sudan is not a State party to the Statute, its refusal to cooperate with the Court was referred to the Security Council.[108] This was in fact the first case of non-cooperation that had been the subject of proceedings before the Court. Upon receipt of this information on the refusal of these States to cooperate, the Council had not taken any concrete measures.

Encounter?", *op. cit.*, p. 63; SCHABAS, W. A., *An introduction to the International Criminal Court*, 2nd ed., New York, CUP, 2004, p. 130.

[107] *Situation in Darfour, The Procureur v. Omar Hassan Ahmad Al Bashir ("Omar Al Bashir")*, ICC-02/05-01/09, Decision Pursuant to Article 87(7) of the Rome Statute on the Failure by the Republic of Malawi to Comply with the Cooperation Requests Issued by the Court with Respect to the Arrest and Surrender of Omar Hassan Ahmad Al Bashir (12 December 2011) (ICC, Pre-Trial Chamber I); ICC-02/05-01/09-140-tENG, Decision pursuant to article 87(7) of the Rome Statute on the refusal of the Republic of Chad to comply with the cooperation requests issued by the Court with respect to the arrest and surrender of Omar Hassan Ahmad Al Bashir (13 December 2011) (ICC, Pre-Trial Chamber I); ICC-02/05-01/09-267, Decision on the non-compliance by the Republic of Uganda with the request to arrest and surrender Omar Al-Bashir to the Court and referring the matter to the United Nations Security Council and the Assembly of State Parties to the Rome Statute (11 July 2016) (ICC, Pre-Trial Chamber II); ICC-02/05-01/09-266, Decision on the non-compliance by the Republic of Djibouti with the request to arrest and surrender Omar Al-Bashir to the Court and referring the matter to the United Nations Security Council and the Assembly of the State Parties to the Rome Statute (11 July 2016) (ICC, Pre-Trial Chamber II).

[108] *The Procureur v. Ahmad Muhammad Harun (Ahmad Harun) et Ali Muhammad Ali Abd-Al-Rahman (Ali Kushayb)*, ICC-02/05-01/07, Decision informing the United Nations Security Council about the lack of cooperation by the Republic of the Sudan (25 May 2010) (ICC, Pre-Trial Chamber I).

Philippe Weckel noted in this connection that « [c]*ompter sur le Conseil de sécurité pour améliorer le respect par les États de leurs obligations de coopérer avec la CPI est vain actuellement, compte tenu du poids négatif qui pèse sur cet organe et impacte son activité bien au-delà de l'exercice du droit de veto* »[109]. Without totally questioning the stance of this author, it is argued that the Security Council was certainly aware of the fact that there is no legal obligation for Chad, Djibouti, Malawi and Uganda to arrest and surrender of a person (Omar Al Bashir) enjoying immunities in accordance with international law. Since the latter was the President-in-Office at the time, he enjoyed immunities before the national courts. It could not be otherwise because the ICJ recognized the validity of the immunities of the Minister of Foreign Affairs before the courts of a foreign State, even when they exercise their universal jurisdiction in the prosecution of international crimes.[110]

3. Legal Grounds for Refusal to Cooperate with the ICC

As per the Rome Statute, requests for cooperation may be denied: (i) based on the existence of a fundamental legal principle of general application in the requested State,[111] (ii) to protect national security,[112] (iii) if the assistance requires the requested State to violate obligations under international law concerning the diplomatic immunity of a person or property of a third State[113].[114]. The grounds for African States' refusal

---

109 WECKEL, P., « L'insuffisante coopération des États à la justice pénale internationale », *Sentinelle*, Bulletin 499, 8 January 2017.

110 *Arrest Warrant of 11 April 2000 (Democratic Republic of the Congo v. Belgium)*, Judgment of 14 February 2022, I.C.J. Reports 2002, p. 3, § 59.

111 Art. 93(3)

112 Art. 72, 93(4) and 93(5).

113 Art. 98(1).

114 BASSIOUNI, M. C., and SCHABAS, W. A., (eds.), *The Legislative History of the International Criminal Court*, 2nd ed., vol. 1, Leiden / Boston, Brill Nijhoff, 2016, p. 212.

to cooperate with the ICC are analysed here in relation to the *Al-Bashir* case. In the context of this case, these grounds can be drawn both from the rules of international law relating to the immunities of State officials and from the African regional derogatory law.

3.1. Rules of International Law Relating to Immunities of State Officials

Customary international law provides protection for State officials through immunities. In this respect, the immunity of Heads of State is based on *comitas gentium*, i.e. the mutual respect of each State towards the representatives of other States. The latter embody the sovereignty of the State and are therefore, according to the theory of the individual-organ, merged with the State.[115] Hans Kelsen formulated this theory in 1943.[116] In its case against France, Djibouti took up this theory in the following terms:

> a State cannot regard a person enjoying the status of an organ of another State as individually criminally liable for acts carried out in that official capacity, that is to say in the performance of his duties. Such acts, indeed, are to be regarded in international law as attributable to the State on behalf of which the organ acted and not to the individual acting as the organ.[117]

According to Jean Salmon, in addition to the exercise of functions, the concept of representation is the basis for the

---

[115] As per Art. 2(1)(b)(iv) of United Nations Convention on Jurisdictional Immunities of States and Their Property, "State" means "representatives of the State acting in that capacity."

[116] KELSEN, H., "Collective and Individual Responsibility in International Law with Particular Regard to the Punishment of War Criminals", *California Law Review*, vol. 31, No. 5, 1943, pp. 530-571 (spec. pp. 533 *et seq.*).

[117] See *Certain Questions of Mutual Assistance in Criminal Matters (Djibouti v. France)*, Judgment, I.C.J. Reports 2008, p. 177, § 187.

principle of immunity of certain senior State officials (Head of State, Prime Minister, and Minister of foreign affairs).[118]

Although Article 11 (1) (b) of the Resolution of the Institute of International Law of 26 August 2001 specifies that "[n]othing in this Resolution may be understood to detract from [...] the obligations under the statutes of the international criminal tribunals as well as the obligations, for those States that have become parties thereto, under the Rome Statute for an International Criminal Court",[119] the exception to the immunity of State officials in general and of the Head of State in particular lacks a solid foundation in international law. In fact, Omar Al-Bashir's multiple trips across Africa and Asia following the ICC's arrest warrants against him are a demonstration of the willingness of the States concerned to respect the immunities of the sitting Head of State.

At the African regional level, Article 46A *bis* of the Statute of the African Court of Justice and Human and Peoples' Rights[120] provides for the immunities of Heads of State or Government and similar state officials as follows: "*No charges shall be commenced or continued before the Court against any serving Au Head of State or Government, or anybody acting or entitled to in such capacity, or other senior state officials based on their functions, during their tenure of office.*"

In this respect, some commentators suggest that:

118 SALMON, J., « Libres propos sur l'arrêt de la CIJ du 14 février 2002 dans l'affaire relative au *Mandat d'arrêt du 11 avril 2000 (RDC c. Belgique)* », *Revue Belge de Droit International*, vol. 35, No. 1-2, 2002, p. 512.

119 *Institut de Droit International*, Session of Vancouver - 2001, Thirteenth Commission, Rapporteur: Mr Joe Verhoeven, Resolution of 26 August 2001 on Immunities from Jurisdiction and Execution of Heads of State and of Government in International Law.

120 Protocol on Amendments to the Protocol on the Statute of the African Court of Justice and Human Rights (the Malabo Protocol) of 27 June 2014.

> it does not follow that the implementation of such an immunity in a regional court would deter offenders; indeed, it could potentially cause leaders to retain power at any cost. It must also be noted that the immunity provided by the African Court may not prevent the ICC from investigating and prosecuting the African Court's members. For example, if the Malabo Protocol were to be implemented and the implementing states had been parties to the Rome Statute but had withdrawn their membership, they could still be investigated and prosecuted for offences committed during their ICC membership period under Article 127(2).[121]

While some authors have argued that international law should not grant immunity to state acts that constitute serious violations of international law and *jus cogens* rules,[122] the consistent and majority practice seems to favour respect for state jurisdictional immunities in all circumstances. It should be recalled that in the *Arrest Warrant* case, although without expressly mentioning the notion of *jus cogens*, the ICJ held that "*there exists under customary international law any form of exception to the rule according immunity from criminal jurisdiction and inviolability to incumbent Ministers for Foreign Affairs, where they are suspected of having committed war crimes or crimes against humanity*".[123] Although this position of the ICJ remains doctrinally controversial, it

---

[121] MBENGUE, M. M., and MCCLELLAN, K., "The ICC and Africa: Should the Latter Remain Engaged?", *Ethiopian Yearbook of International Law*, 2018, vol. 2017, p. 187-203 (spec. pp. 199-200).

[122] COSTI, A., « L'arrêt de la Cour internationale de Justice dans l'affaire des immunités juridictionnelles de l'État », *Quebec Journal of International Law*, Special Issue, June 2015 (*Mélanges en l'honneur de Jacques-Yvan Morin*), pp. 267-311 (spec. p. 274, note 55). L'auteur argues that « *la Cour* [a] *emprunt*[é] *une approche conservatrice à l'égard de la relation entre l'immunité de l'État et les violations de normes impératives de droit international coutumier auxquelles aucune dérogation n'est permise (règles de* jus cogens*). En effet, elle rejette l'existence d'une exception à l'immunité juridictionnelle de l'État même dans les cas de violations graves du droit international humanitaire* » (pp. 268-269).

[123] *Arrest Warrant of 11 April 2000 (Democratic Republic of the Congo v. Belgium)*, *op. cit.*, § 58.

has « *l'avantage de la clarté et d'avoir été approuvée par une forte majorité (treize conte trois)* ».[124]

In the *Jurisdictional Immunities of the State* case, the ICJ decided by a majority that Italy had violated German immunity under international law by allowing civil suits in its courts and by taking enforcement measures against property owned by Germany, as well as by having Greek courts decisions recognised in Italy on the basis of the same arguments.[125] According to Paula Wojcikiewicz Almeida, who is highly critical of the ICJ's reasoning in this case, by adopting this position the Court has avoided confronting the thorny conflict involving State immunity and the violation of *jus cogens* rules, by rejecting the idea of an emerging exception to State immunity.[126]

It is worth noting that « [l]*e défaut de pertinence de la qualité officielle* [qui] *est un héritage reconduit sur les trois générations des juridictions internationales pénales depuis le Tribunal International Militaire de Nuremberg jusqu'à la CPI en passant par les tribunaux mixtes* » [127] is struggling to take hold in state practice. The same is true of Article 98(2) of the Rome Statute. Indeed, the analysis of the ICC's requests for arrest and surrender highlights « *la difficulté sur plusieurs années de mettre en œuvre les*

---

124 HENZELIN, M., « L'immunité pénale des ministres selon la Cour internationale de justice », *Revue Pénale Suisse*, vol. 120, 2002, pp. 249-264 (spec. p. 252).

125 *Jurisdictional Immunities of the State (Germany v. Italy: Greece intervening)*, Judgment of 3 February 2012, I.C.J. Reports 2012, p. 99, §§ 107, 120, 131, 133 and 139.

126 WOJCIKIEWICZ ALMEIDA, P., « L'affaire des immunités juridictionnelles de l'État (Allemagne c. Italie) : la Cour internationale de Justice à contre-sens de l'évolution du droit international », *ACDI - Anuario Colombiano de Derecho Internacional*, vol. 11, 2018, pp. 21-70 (spec. pp. 26-27).

127 BADUGUE, P.L., « L'exécution des mandats internationaux de la Cour pénale internationale contre les chefs d'État en exercice : jusqu'où va l'obligation de coopérer des États parties ? Entre l'indifférence pénale à la qualité officielle de la Cour et l'objection des États », *eRIDP*, 2018, p. 2.

obligations découlant du Statut de Rome, notamment lorsque l'indifférence de la Cour à l'égard des immunités rencontre la sensibilité des États à celles de leurs dirigeants ».[128]

In its declaratory statement on the decision to withdraw from the Rome Statute of the ICC, South Africa stated, among other reasons, that it "*requested th*[e] *Assembly of State Parties to clarify the nature and scope of the provisions of Article 98 of the Rome Statue and its relationship with Article 27. It is disconcerting that there was opposition to this proposal as there are fundamental differences on the issue of immunities of Heads of State*".[129] It is worth recalling that the decision on the ICC, taken during the 30th Ordinary Session of the AU Assembly of Heads of State and Government, requested:

> the African Group in New York to immediately place on the agenda of the United Nations General Assembly a request to seek an advisory opinion from the International Court of Justice on the question of immunities of a Head of State and Government and other Senior Officials as it relates to the relationship between Articles 27 and 98 and the obligations of States Parties under International Law.[130]

The following year AU Assembly called upon "*the ICC to respect the duty of all States Parties to the Rome Statute to honour their other international obligations as stipulated in Article 98, which includes the right to host international meetings and to ensure the participation of all invited delegations and high officials*".[131] Even if an international

---

[128] *Ibid.*, p. 1.

[129] C.N.786.2016.TREATIES-XVIII.10 (Depositary Notification) of 25 October 2016 (South Africa: Withdrawal), p. 3, https://treaties.un.org/doc/Publication/CN/2016/CN.786.2016-Eng.pdf (visited 22 October 2022).

[130] AU Assembly, 30th Ordinary Session of the Assembly, 28- 29 January 2018, Addis Ababa, Ethiopia, Decision on the International Criminal Court, Doc. EX.CL/1068(XXXII), § 5(ii). This decision "suggests that African states want to remain engaged with international courts and tribunals." See MBENGUE, M.M., and MCCLELLAN, K., "The ICC and Africa: Should the Latter Remain Engaged?", *op. cit.*, p. 201.

[131] AU Assembly, 32nd Ordinary Session of the Assembly, 10- 11 February 2019, Addis Ababa, Ethiopia, Decision on the International Criminal

custom creating an exception to the immunities of the head of state in the event of the commission of international crimes before international criminal tribunals and courts were real,[132] its universality would be questionable, due to the iterative objection of African States and the AU, « *assimilable à une* mutus dissensus *(interprétation authentique commune contre une norme) susceptible d'amender toute norme internationale contraire* ».[133] African States have rightly refused to cooperate in the execution of the arrest warrants issued against Omar Al-Bashir.

3.2. The Conflicting African Regional Law

African regional law conflicting with African States' obligations to cooperate with the ICC is also a basis for the refusal of these States to cooperate in the arrest and surrender of a sitting African Head of State. As Mouangue Kobila noted, the AU's decisions not to cooperate in the execution of the arrest warrants issued against the then Sudanese and Libyan presidents essentially raised the problem of the relationship between the universal legal order and the African regional legal order.[134] The question arises as to the place of African regionalism in the relationship between the universal legal order and the national legal order. As an author noted, « *le régionalisme apparaît avec constance comme une forme permanente de revendication et traduit une forme de 'militantisme juridique' source de 'doctrines continentales' tendant à souligner le particularisme de certains*

Court, Doc. EX.CL/1138(XXXIV), § 6.

132 It is what the Pre-Trial Chamber I stated in its Decision Pursuant to Article 87(7) of the Rome Statute on the Failure by the Republic of Malawi to Comply with the Cooperation Requests Issued by the Court with Respect to the Arrest and Surrender of Omar Hassan Ahmad Al Bashir, *op. cit.*, para. 43.

133 KOBILA, J. M., « L'Afrique et les juridictions internationales pénales », *op. cit.*, p. 21.

134 *Ibid.*, p. 5.

régimes internationaux, à l'exemple du régionalisme latino-américain ou de ce que l'on peut hâtivement appeler le régionalisme africain »[135].

The refusal of African States to cooperate highlights the conflict between ICC law and AU law. Article 30 of the Vienna Convention on the Law of Treaties cannot apply to resolution of the conflict of norms in this case, as there is no question of successive treaties on the same subject matter. Instead, the principle of *lex specialis derogat generali* (special law prevails over general law) seems appropriate. In the relationship between the AU and the ICC, the derogatory force of the *lex specialis* should, in all likelihood, benefit the AU, « *dans la mesure où les normes et appréciations d'une organisation régionale relèvent incontestablement en droit positif de la* lex specialis *du point de vue géographique, aussi bien relativement à la CPI que relativement aux Nations Unies qui sont des structures universelles* »[136]. Curiously, Bokhe Murungu believes that the AU's decision to ask all African member States of the organisation not to cooperate with the ICC in the arrest and surrender of Omar Al-Bashir was a violation of its own Constitutive Act, in particular Article 4(h), (m) and (o).[137] In contrast to this opinion, in the event of a conflict between a multilateral agreement, even a later one, and a regional integration treaty, Marcus-Helmons suggests the application of the principle of pre-eminence of the integration treaty.[138] As far as Europe is concerned, an author admits that the resolution of conflicts

---

135 DOUMBE-BILLE, S., « Propos introductifs », in Stéphane DOUMBE-BILLE (ed.), *La régionalisation du droit international*, Bruxelles, Bruylant, 2012, pp. 10-17 (spec. p. 13).

136 MOUANGUE KOBILA, J., « L'Afrique et les juridictions internationales pénales », *op. cit.*, p. 49.

137 BOKHE MURUNGU, C., *Immunity of State Officials and Prosecution of International Crimes in Africa*, PhD Thesis, Faculty of Law, University of Pretoria, 2011, p. 286.

138 MARCUS-HELMONS, S., « Les effets en droit communautaire d'un accord international conclu par un des États membres des communautés en violation d'un engagement antérieur », *Revue Belge de Droit International*, No. 2, 1962, pp. 379-402 (spec. p. 387).

of international norms requires a hierarchy between international and European law, even if « *chaque système, en se repliant sur lui-même, adopte une démarche strictement interne, marquant ainsi sa préférence pour ses solutions propres* »[139].

If one looks at the sources of the conflicting obligations of African States, namely the Rome Statute, on the one hand, and the decisions of the AU Assembly of Heads of State and Government, on the other, one could conclude that the obligations to the ICC have primacy, as the Rome Statute is a treaty with a higher legal value than the decisions or resolutions of the AU's deliberative organ. However, if one goes further to simply compare the Court's requests for cooperation with AU decisions, it is clear that the latter would prevail over the former, as the AU is a regional integration organisation.

Conclusion

This article set out the legal basis of both the obligation and refusal to cooperate of African States with the ICC. First, the obligation to cooperate is examined based on the relevant provisions of the Rome Statute. In this respect, the article postulates that it is an obligation principally borne by States Parties though specific provisions of the Statute state the obligation to cooperate of third States: Article 12(3) (case of acceptance of the Court's jurisdiction), article 13(b) (case of referral of a situation to the of office of the prosecutor by the Security Council). Second, the obligation to cooperate can be created through *ad hoc* cooperation arrangements or agreements concluded by the Court and Non-Party States. A State that concludes such an instrument is under an obligation similar to that of States Parties. The article also assesses the incorporation of the obligation to cooperate in eight African

139 BERGE, J. S., « Interactions du droit international et du droit européen. Approche du phénomène en trois étapes dans le contexte européen », *JDI*, July-August-September 2009, pp. 903-922 (spec. p. 917).

States Parties' laws, exposing their diversity as regards the imperative nature of this obligation. In addition, the article points out that the ICC lacks coercive power against requested States that fail to provide it assistance. In the last section of the article, legal grounds for refusal of African States to cooperate with the Court are discussed in relation to the *Al-Bashir* case. It is postulated that two main reasons could justify the denial of assistance in the arrest and surrender of Al-Bashir, that is, rules of international law relating to immunities of State officials and the conflicting African regional law (AU law). Indeed, the arrest and surrender of the then Sudanese president required African States to violate their obligations under international law concerning the immunity of a sitting Head of State. As far as the conflict of laws is concerned, regional law (AU law) shall prevail over a multilateral treaty (Rome Statute). Therefore, despite criticism of the Court's African bias, in the *Al-Bashir* case African States used legal arguments to deny assistance to the Court.

Effects of east african community integration on trade: the case study of Uganda

By

Gregory Fah Fombo

Department of Political Science, University of Bamenda and Department of International Relations and Conflict Resolution, University of Buea

Maurine Gloria Kawona

Finn Church Aid, Uganda

and

Kiven James Kewir

Department of Political Science and Comparative Politics, University of Buea, Guest Lecturer, Department of Political Science, University of Bamenda

E mail: jameskewir@yahoo.com

Abstract

This study sets out to examine the views of Ugandan business elites on the impact of regional integration on Uganda's trade within the East African Community (EAC) and reflects on how membership in parallel regional economic communities (RECs) impinges on integration rewards for Uganda. Specifically, the views of business elites on the impact of the Customs Union and Economic Union treaties put in place by EAC states have contributed to removing tariff and non-tariff barriers to the free movement of goods and services between member countries. The study employed a qualitative research approach. Semi-structured interviews were conducted with Ugandan business men and women to elicit their views on the impact of EAC integration on tariff and non-tariff barriers to trade in Uganda. It shows that Ugandan business elites believe EAC trade integration has reduced tariff and non-tariff barriers to trade but that significant tariff restrictions remain and need to be addressed. Participants also believed that successful implementation of relevant treaties will significantly boost Uganda's intra-EAC trade. The main obstacles identified are; multiple memberships, poor funding of regional agencies concerned with implementation of relevant treaties and the persistence of a few specific protectionist practices targeting imports from member states. Ongoing efforts to coordinate inter-economic community trade rules offers a vista for a wider community, which will be of even greater benefits to Uganda and other member countries.

Key Words: Customs union, trade integration, multiple membership, tariffs

Introduction

In the last three decades, the phenomenon of regional trade integration has experienced a significant and constant increase. Most countries in the world are either members or in a process of creating or joining a regional trade scheme[1].Africa has not been an exception to this development. The Economic Commission for Africa (ECA) became the champion of regional integration in the mid-1960s and proposed the division of Africa into regions for the purpose of economic development[2]. That proposal has been heeded and better articulated in the Lagos Plan of Action. Current African integration arrangements can be divided into two broad groups: those that fit into the Lagos Plan of Action (LPA) adopted in April 1980, and those that were either in existence or came about outside the LPA.

The LPA was promoted by ECA and launched in a special initiative by the OAU. It envisaged three regional arrangements aimed at the creation of separate but convergent and overreaching integration arrangements in three sub-Saharan sub-regions. In West Africa, there was the Economic Community of West African States (ECOWAS) which, pre-dated the Lagos Plan. A Preferential Trade Area (PTA) was established in 1981 to cover the countries of East and Southern Africa, which was eventually replaced in 1993 by the Common Market for Eastern and Southern Africa (COMESA). For Central Africa the treaty of the Economic Community of Central African States (ECCAS) was approved in 1983 but remains to be fully ratified. Together with the

---

[1] UNECA, *Assessing regional integration in Africa III: towards monetary and financial integration in Africa*, United Nations Publications, 2008

[2] Matthews, A., Regional Integration and Food Security in Developing Countries, Food and Agricultural Organization of the United Nations (FAO), Rome, 2003, p. 73

Arab Maghreb Union (AMU) in North Africa, these arrangements were expected to lead to an all-African common market by the year 2025. The Lagos Plan was followed up in 1991 by the Abuja Treaty, re-affirming the commitment of the OAU's Heads of State to an integrated African economy.[3] This vision remained following the launch of the African Union in April 2001, by African Heads of State, at Sirte to replace the OAU.

A second group of integration arrangements has grown up outside the LPA. Two important RTAs are associated with the former CFA zone. There is the West African Economic and Monetary Union (WAEMU) within the ambit of ECOWAS and the Economic and Monetary Union of Central Africa (CEMAC) within the proposed ECCAS region. Within the geographic area of COMESA there are the Southern African Customs Union (SACU) with its associated monetary union (the Common Monetary Area, CMA), the Southern African Development Community (SADC) and the East African Community (EAC). Some countries in this region are also joined with countries in the Horn of Africa in the Intergovernmental Authority on Development (IGAD)[4].

Uganda as a member of the East African Community (EAC) is the focus of the paper. The EAC is a regional intergovernmental organization of Burundi, Kenya, Rwanda, Uganda and the United Republic of Tanzania with its Headquarters in Arusha, Tanzania. Early attempts at forming an East African Community between Kenya, Tanzania and Uganda started in 1967 and failed in 1977 as the three countries could not agree on a number of important economic and political issues. However, it was later

---

[3] UNECA, *Assessing regional integration in Africa III: towards monetary and financial integration in Africa*, United Nations Publications, 2008

[4] Mwapachu, J., Challenging the Frontiers of African Integration.The Dynamics of Policies, Politics and Transformation in the East African Community.*E&D Vision Publishing, Dar es Salaam,* 2012

rejuvenated in 1999 and as of 2007, Rwanda and Burundi joined the East Africa community[5].

The Treaty establishing the East African Community was signed on 30th November 1999 and entered into force on 7th July 2000, following its ratification by the original Three Partner States – Kenya, Uganda and Tanzania. The Republic of Rwanda and the Republic of Burundi acceded to the EAC Treaty on 18th June 2007 and became full Members of the Community with effect from 1st July 2007[6]. The aim of the EAC is to deepen co-operation among the partner states in political, economic, social and other fields for their mutual benefit. To further economic cooperation among member states, the EAC countries established a Customs Union in 2005 and a Common Market in the year 2012. Behind all this is a bigger ambition for the EAC to become a political federation as is cited in the EAC protocol.

In theory, the elimination of barriers to trade through free movement of factors of production like labour and capital encourages countries to trade more with others in the integration scheme. However, since the revitalization of the EAC on 30th November 1999, Uganda appears not to have benefitted significantly from trade with other EAC states. The purpose of this research was thus to examine the impact of integration on trade between Uganda and other EAC countries from the perspective of Ugandan businessmen. A qualitative research approach was adopted. Qualitative data was collected using semi-structured interviews. Participants, who were both male and female, were selected using the snowball sampling technique in Kampala and Entebbe. The

---

[5] Kasasira, R., *East Africa: Rwanda, Burundi to Sign EAC Treaty in Kampala*, 2007, Accessed on 1st June, 2015 from http://allafrica.com/stories/200706110105.html

[6].ibid Kasasira, 2007

main criteria for selection were to have knowledge and experience of cross-border trade in the EAC.

After the foregoing introduction, the rest of the paper is structured as follows; section two discusses the theoretical framework, the third section examines the benefits and achievements of the EAC, the fourth section discusses the obstacles and opportunities for intra-EAC trade while the last section is a conclusion.

1. Theoretical framework

This paper uses customs union theory as the framework for analysis. Although other theories have been advanced to explain the phenomenon of economic integration, the customs union theory remains relevant in understanding the phenomenon.

The Customs Union (CU) is defined as the process of "elimination of intra-trade barriers and the equalization of tariffs on imports from non-member countries[7]. CU theory examines markets and goods within a region and the effect of discrimination within the integrating area. Jacob Viner[8], and Maurice Byé[9] all published works that analysed the welfare implications of establishing a customs union on the world, but it is Jacob Viner that is widely recognised as the father of the customs union theory. Richard Lipsey[10] has summarised the reasoning concerning customs unions before Viner as follows:

---

[7] Viner, J., "The Customs Union Issue" New York: Carnegie Endowment for International Peace, 1950

[8] Ibid

[9] Bye, M. "Customs Unions and National Interests, International Economic Papers No. 3, 1954

[10] Richard, L., " The Theory of Customs Unions: A General Survey." *Economic Journal*, 70, 1960, p. 497

> Free trade maximises world welfare; a customs union reduces tariffs and is therefore a movement towards free trade; a customs union will, therefore, increase world welfare even if it does not lead to a world welfare maximum.

In *The Customs Union Issue,* Viner showed this argument to be incorrect. He argued that the benefits of economic integration were not self-evident, and world welfare would increase only under certain conditions. He demonstrated this by introducing the concepts of trade creation and trade diversion.[11] According to Viner, participating countries and the world at large benefit from a customs union, if the trade-creating forces are predominant, but both the participating countries as well as the world at large suffer, if the trade-diverting forces are predominant.[12]

The primary effect of a customs union is the expansion of trade flows among member countries, often at the expense of trade with non-members. The expansion is a consequence of the removal of the intra-union tariff barriers and can be decomposed into trade creation (more efficient suppliers in CU partners replace domestic suppliers of a given good) and trade diversion (more efficient third-party suppliers are displaced by less efficient suppliers located in partner countries, as a result of the discriminatory liberalisation).

Viner's study was the first to identify concrete criteria to distinguish between the possible advantages and disadvantages of economic integration (benefits and challenges). Viner clearly points out that regional trade agreement does not necessarily result in gains to members, even though some tariffs are eliminated by the agreement. Rather, he argues that the creation of a CU may result in either trade creation or trade diversion and that trade creation improves the country's welfare while trade diversion lowers it. Trade is created within an integrating area when the output of

[11] Ibid Viner, 1950

[12] Viner, 1950, op. cit. p. 44

inefficient producers is replaced after the elimination of tariffs by cheaper imports from more efficient producers within the region to the benefit of both producers and consumers.

On the other hand, trade diversion effect occurs when the imposition of common external tariff puts suppliers from countries outside the integrating area in a competitive disadvantage by encouraging imports from less efficient suppliers within the union. Thus, this condition leads to trade diversion which reduces the economic welfare and benefits accruable to members of the union. Viner concluded that, participating countries and the world at large benefit from a customs union, if the trade-creating forces are predominant, but both the participating countries as well as the world at large suffer, if the trade-diverting forces are predominant[13].

The main criticism of the application of Vinerian theory to understanding of economic integration in the developing world has been that the volume of goods that these countries can produce and exchange among themselves is small and that tariffs have not been a major obstacle to trade[14]. These arguments do not however make the theory of customs unions irrelevant in understanding the phenomenon of economic integration in the developing world. Trade among less developed countries, particularly in Africa has remained largely informal and African countries have embarked on economic integration projects largely because of the perceived benefits identified by CU theory and generally market integration scholars.

The East African Community established and implemented a common external tariff (CET) applied by all members of EAC against goods entering the region. The establishment of CET was also accompanied by the gradual reduction of the common internal tariff. The purpose of

---

[13] Viner, J , 1950, p. 44 Op.cit

[14] Ravenhill, J., 1980, quoted in Østergaard 1993, 33

creating the EAC customs union and common market has been to increase the volume of trade among members and ultimately the welfare of participating states. Customs union theory therefore provides a good framework for analysis.

2. Benefits and Achievements of EAC integration

Participants were asked whether following the various responses on whether or not Uganda's intra EAC trade has increased since the creation of the customs union by EAC states in 2005. Most participants were of the view that their trade has been facilitated by customs union procedures such as the one stop tax payment at the borders of member states. One participant for example said "the customs union has led to uniform trade tariffs and policies on goods imported from EAC countries which have led to trade creation as it is easy to switch from a high-cost supplier to a low-cost supplier in another member country". This participant also holds that the customs union has spearheaded competition between domestic and foreign firms that are specializing on one product to gain comparative advantage which has led to the increase in output and a decline in the prices and production efficiency. Another participant was of the view that volume of exports from Uganda to countries like Rwanda and South Sudan has increased.

Although all participants were of the opinion that the volume of trade has increased as a result of the creation of the CU, they could not clearly say to what extent it has affected trade. Participants were nonetheless unanimous that the overall increase is smaller than expected due to challenges to the full operationalization of the customs union, such as the differences in tax regimes between EAC countries.

- Several reasons were advanced by respondents to explain why they believed trade has been created as a result of the putting in place of a CU by the EAC. The main reasons according to participants were;

- Benefits in terms of waivers of some taxes as incentive for doing business within the community
- It is easy to predict the economic environment thus aiding planning for the better and shoddier economic conditions
- It is also an opportunity to trade with investors in the wider markets than previously small individual local markets.
- Unique calibration of some goods like soda ash, machinery and lubricants
- The cost of goods within the community is relatively affordable such as soda ash from Kenya.
- Trade facilitation has improved through SCT (Scanner Technology) and AEO (Authorized Economic Operators), simplification of documentation, shortening the process of clearing goods and education on the importation procedures by the tax bodies.
- Non-Tariff Trade Barrier complaints are addressed immediately and harmonization of the certificates of origin.
- Some products such as textiles are more accessible and purchased at a cheaper price than before within the community, and so it is efficient and effective to trade within the region.
- Closer business associates thus easy business networking
- Trust and honesty because of the knowledge of the people from the same region

In spite of these, a few participants were critical, arguing that although trade has increased, gains for Uganda pale out in comparison to those of Kenya. According to these participants, there have been more imports from Kenya into Uganda. Another respondent John provides tabular evidence below indicating that Uganda has not benefited from the EAC integration following the volume of exports. The goods imported from Kenya were however considered by most participants to be those for which the country had a comparative advantage in and a reason why trade could be said to have been created.

These benefits were believed not to be sufficiently enjoyed since the creation of the CU. Participants were very critical of the achievements of the EAC. One participant said little had been done to effectively put in place common standards for certification in Kenya and Tanzania, immigration and customs procedures.[15]

Although the CU was considered to have led to an increase in trade with other member states, participants believed the volumes were below expectation. One participant for example said: "since the creation of the EAC, there should have been a significant increase in trade among member states, but surprisingly Uganda still does lots of trade with the EU, America and Middle Eastern countries than it does with the EAC states"[16].

The findings show that the creation of the CU has increased trade and that there has been little or no trade diversion because member states produce and exchange goods for which they have a comparative advantage. This supports the argument of customs union theory that welfare increases when the more efficient producer falls within the integrated area. Although member states such as Uganda continue to have more imports from non-member states, these imports are mostly manufactured goods for which members do not produce or are less efficient in producing.

---

15 Interview in Entebbe, June 2015

16 Interview in Kampala, June 2015

3. Obstacles and Opportunities for Intra - EAC trade

Participants identified several obstacles impeding the full implementation of the customs union. The main challenges identified included: the similarity of goods, weak political will, the participation of members in other regional groupings, near absence of leadership and non-tariff barriers.

One participant was of the opinion that the "Similarity of products is an obstacle since governments in the EAC countries still find it a duty to protect their own countries. An example is the standoff that erupted between Uganda and Kenya when Kenya refused the import of chicken from Uganda"[17]. Another participant similarly said " to a large extent the similarity of national products can be regarded as an obstacle to developing intra- trade among EAC member states. This is because different EAC States have different labour endowments and technological development. Therefore under developed countries like Uganda with lower level of commercial productivity will specialize in goods whose production is intensive in unskilled labour, thus lower quality goods, hence causing local producers in Uganda to loose trade as compared to their counterparts with advanced technology achieving higher capital gains as a result of the union"[18]. Another participant argued that "Most of the products are agricultural commodities, coffee, flowers, food, live animals, beverages, tobacco and inedible crude materials. The obstacle here is that no country will like to buy what they produce".[19]

Most participants however believed that similarities of products was not an issue because to them, "the market is large enough to take all products."[20] These participants rather

[17] Interview in Kampala, June 2015
[18] Interview in Kampala, June 2015
[19] Interview in Entebe, June 2015
[20] Interview in Kampala, June 2015

saw harmonization of customs procedures to be critical for the EAC trade.

Non-tariff barriers according to participants constituted another major challenge. Among these were the existence of multiple roadblocks in Kenya and Tanzania, "which hinder fast movement of goods between countries and have especially fostered corruption, which increases the cost of transactions". Additionally, delays with customs procedures were also highlighted. The waits at the Tanzanian border were described by some as "stressful" and "difficult to cope with"[21]. One participant said the Tanzania Food and Drug authority still imposes requirements on food and cosmetics from Uganda, making it difficult for Ugandan businesses to export there.

The problem of non-tariff barriers has been significantly addressed in the literature. Viljoen observed that the movement of goods is also not as straight forward as it should be in a CU, with complaints of non-tariff barriers such as police and immigration checks faced by transporters of goods across the partner states.[22] Accusations and counteraccusations by these states corroborate the observations of this author. EAC partner states in 2012/2013 accused each other of introducing new barriers to trade by imposing novel cargo transit fees. Kenya accused Tanzania of introducing such fees at the Arusha border, and similarly, Tanzanian transporters have decried an increase in transit fees for trucks crossing over from Rwanda into Tanzania, from $152 to $500. [23]

---

[21] Interview in Entebbe, June 2015

[22] Viljoen, W., Non-tariff barriers affecting trade in the COMESA- EAC-SADC Tripartite Free
Trade Agreement, Working Paper, Trade Law Centre for Southern Africa, 2011

[23] Tumwebaze.P., Rwanda moves to harmonise transit charges with Tanzania, 2013,
http://www.newtimes.co.rw/news/index.php?i=15471&a=70136

Another obstacle identified by all participants was the near absence of effective leadership in the region. One participant for example said that "some of the issues agreed upon at the presidential level have not yet trickled down to the operational level because of weak leadership."[24] They averred that effective leadership is necessary to address the problems of red-tape and low computerization of customs procedures.

Multiple memberships of some EAC countries in several other trade integration schemes was also considered by participants to be a key obstacle which led to low commitment to the EAC protocols. Tanzania, for example, is perceived to be hesitant on harmonising trade policies due to its membership in the SADC[25]. The question of overlapping membership has been examined in the literature. Both, Kenya and Uganda are members of the EAC, COMESA and IGAD. Similarly, Tanzania is a member of the EAC and SADC though not IGAD. [26] This has led to conflicting mandates as exporters must comply with various tariff reduction schedules, rules of origin and other liberalization requirements and duplication of policies and programmes. It also imposes undue administrative and financial cost to the partner states.

Tanzania, as a member of both the Southern African Development Community (SADC) and the EAC, has taken integration commitments in both regional contexts, thereby having to implement two CET, one being for EAC and the other for SADC. All other members of the EAC are also members of the Common Market for Eastern and Southern Africa (COMESA), thus facing similar challenges as the one

---

[24] Interview in Kampala, June 20215

[25] Interview in Kampala, June 2015

[26] It withdrew its membership from the COMESA in favour of the southern African RTA, SADC.

encountered by Tanzania in terms of multiple commitments taken in the contexts of various integration agenda[27].

Since each regional community has tended to develop its own trade regime (for example SADC has a very different set of rules of origin governing the granting of trade preferences to that of COMESA), the membership in multiple agreements often entails applying differing trade rules to different regional partners. This hampers trade flows by raising the costs involved for traders in meeting multiple sets of trade rules and gives rise to inconsistencies in the rules and procedures applied by the different trade agreements, distorting regional markets and causing severe problems of effective implementation.[28] The difficulties posed by these was captured by a participant who said "member states joining other customs agreements do not favour trade among the EAC, simply because it adds to the complexity of things to deal with in harmonizing and creating favourable trade policies..[29]"

In an effort to ride the challenge posed by multiple membership in diverse economic groupings, a tripartite summit of the Heads of State and Government of COMESA, SADC and EAC countries was held in Kampala, Uganda on 22 October 2008. The meeting essentially set out to harmonise the policies of these three RECs and opened up prospects for a larger group. While the promise exists for the 26 member states of these RECs to form one bloc, not much has been realized on the ground to address the problem of overlapping membership. But it is an important step in the

---

[27] Makame, A., The East African integration: Achievement and challenges, *Great Insights*, Volume 1, Issue 6. Maastricht: ECDPM, 2012

[28] World Bank, *Defragmenting Africa: Deepening regional Trade integration in goods and services.* Washington D.C., 2012

[29] Interviewed in Kampala, June 2015

direction of building the African Economic Community envisaged in the Abuja Treaty[30].

Conclusion

The purpose of this study was to investigate views of stakeholders in Uganda on the effects of the EAC customs union on trade, in regard to Uganada and more generally in the subregion. The findings show that although there has been an increase in trade with EAC member states since the creation of the CU, participants believe the benefits remain below expectation. This situation is blamed on members not fully implementing the Custom Union and their divided loyalties emanating from belonging to parallel groups.

The EAC customs union has led to reduced tariff and non-tariff trade barriers which in turn has increased trade and enhanced consumer choice. This is reflected in the reduction of administrative barriers such as customs checks within internal border. However, non-tariff barriers related to trade like administrative and bureaucratic inefficiencies and other indirect tariffs, regulations, and practices at the national and local level that increase the cost of trade still exist. The study thus shows that in spite of the progress made, the pace of operationalization of the CU can be described as slow. This slow pace is explained by several challenges. The most notable challenges identified were; multiple memberships, weak leadership and non-tariff barriers. These challenges can be overcome through effective regional leadership and the coordination of policies between different schemes by member states as is currently being done through initiatives such as the Tripartite Agreement.

---

[30] Hartzenberg, T., Regional Integration in Africa. World Trade Organization Economic Research and Statistics Division. Staff Working Paper ERSD-2011-14, 2011

Structures éditoriales du groupe L'Harmattan

L'Harmattan Italie
Via degli Artisti, 15
10124 Torino
harmattan.italia@gmail.com

L'Harmattan Hongrie
Kossuth l. u. 14-16.
1053 Budapest
harmattan@harmattan.hu

L'Harmattan Sénégal
10 VDN en face Mermoz
BP 45034 Dakar-Fann
senharmattan@gmail.com

L'Harmattan Cameroun
TSINGA/FECAFOOT
BP 11486 Yaoundé
inkoukam@gmail.com

L'Harmattan Burkina Faso
Achille Somé – tengnule@hotmail.fr

L'Harmattan Guinée
Almamya, rue KA 028 OKB Agency
BP 3470 Conakry
harmattanguinee@yahoo.fr

L'Harmattan RDC
185, avenue Nyangwe
Commune de Lingwala – Kinshasa
matangilamusadila@yahoo.fr

L'Harmattan Congo
219, avenue Nelson Mandela
BP 2874 Brazzaville
harmattan.congo@yahoo.fr

L'Harmattan Mali
ACI 2000 - Immeuble Mgr Jean Marie Cisse
Bureau 10
BP 145 Bamako-Mali
mali@harmattan.fr

L'Harmattan Togo
Djidjole – Lomé
Maison Amela
face EPP BATOME
ddamela@aol.com

L'Harmattan Côte d'Ivoire
Résidence Karl – Cité des Arts
Abidjan-Cocody
03 BP 1588 Abidjan
espace_harmattan.ci@hotmail.fr

Nos librairies en France

Librairie internationale
16, rue des Écoles
75005 Paris
librairie.internationale@harmattan.fr
01 40 46 79 11
www.librairieharmattan.com

Librairie des savoirs
21, rue des Écoles
75005 Paris
librairie.sh@harmattan.fr
01 46 34 13 71
www.librairieharmattansh.com

Librairie Le Lucernaire
53, rue Notre-Dame-des-Champs
75006 Paris
librairie@lucernaire.fr
01 42 22 67 13

www.ingramcontent.com/pod-product-compliance
Lightning Source LLC
LaVergne TN
LVHW021218061026
849535LV00008B/2795

* 9 7 8 2 3 3 6 4 3 6 9 4 4 *